What's Up Doc

Dr. Jerry F. Strissel

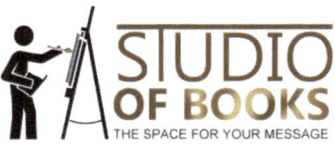

Studio of Books LLC
5900 Balcones Drive Suite 100
Austin, Texas 78731
www.studioofbooks.org
Hotline: (254) 800-1183

Ordering Information:
Special discounts are available on quantity purchases by corporations, associations, and others. For details, contact the publisher at the address above.

Printed in the United States of America.

ISBN-13: Softcover   978-1-964864-76-1
          eBook   978-1-964864-75-4

Library of Congress Control Number: 2024922166

The Author

D r. Jerry "Doc" Strissel grew up on a family farm south of Denison, Iowa and at the age of 10, lost the use of one leg due to the polio epidemic in the early 1950's. It was devasting at the time, but it did start a motivational concept in him that has lasted throughout his lifetime. Finding solutions to everyday issues because of the paralysis became a very positive influence. In addition to creating a positive attitude, there was also an incentive to generate a spark of life in general.

Building and flying model airplanes developed into a major hobby for Doc and after graduating from high school, he attended Iowa State University majoring in Aeronautical Engineering. One year later, a new career choice was made. It was now centered around teaching biology, and it remained that way until graduation. At that time Doc accepted a research position in graduate school. He Received his M.S. and Ph.D. in plant pathology followed by a two-year Iowa State Post Doctorate assignment.

The life of a research scientist became even more interesting after leaving Iowa State University. Doc's first professional employment was with a new upstart company called Environment 2000, LTD. The company's mission was to develop and commercialize a biological control agent to eradicate Salmonella. It was a major threat to the pet turtle industry.

The second upstart company Doc was employed by was called the Dawn Corporation. It was focused on extracting plant growth hormones from kelp. It was originally designed for use in the flower industry, but it also got tested on vegetable crops and then field crops.

To add to his diversified background, Doc became the quality control manager for a company making animal pharmaceutical products for Allied Mills in Chicago, Illinois. During this time, Doc met his future wife, Dorothy Lung from Broomfield, Colorado. They later had three daughters, eleven granddaughters, and two grandsons.

In the fall of 1981, Doc began employment as director of research with Wilson Seeds in Harlan, Iowa. This was the beginning of a fascinating career in the corn world. Through the following years there would be acquisitions, working with scientists from other parts of the world and gaining access to the most diversified set of corn germplasm available independently derived.

Doc developed his own company, JFS and Associates, LTD. in December of 2005 and has traveled throughout the world creating a network of corn breeders from Argentina, Mexico, Turkey, South Africa and the United States. These breeders contribute corn germplasm and ideas to help create new, innovative products for the food industry, animal feed, bourbon, corn oil for aviation fuel, ethanol and the extraction of non-GMO protein from white corn to use in fish farming. The interaction between these people from around the world to create new products and passing that concept on to the next generation of farmers is very important.

Dedication

This book is dedicated to the memory of my late wife and best friend Dorothy, Dorothy's late sisters, Beth and Deborah, my parents, Fritz and Laretta Strissel, all of whom contributed some positive aspect or learning experience to my life.

A very special thank you goes to my three daughters, Vicki, Shannon and Jeri and their families for all the entertainment and for solidifying the concepts I had regarding the values of having a good family foundation.

A special thank you also goes out to my brother Dan who has a terrific memory and who supplied me with a lot of details from the past that I had forgotten or was not aware of at the time. He did supply a lot of entertainment for our family with all his Christmas decorations and supplying a boat for Sunday outings during the summer.

A special thank you also to Jim Bartholomew and his sister Mary Ann for supplying numerous pictures for this book, and the background information pertaining to the events that happened at the Denison Candy Kitchen, and the airplane spraying episodes. Mary Ann also furnished some special editing recommendations.

Another thank you goes to Neila Rohn for compiling a lot of information on the family tree many years ago.

Table of Contents

Preface

The original intent of writing a series of books was to document the life history of the Strissel family from the late 1800's through the present time. However, once I got started, I soon realized that due to my age, I had the privilege of observing many events and trends that had occurred over a long period of time. Several of these events had a direct effect on the way a person's life was headed, and for the most part, it turned out to be an inspiration to accomplish tasks that one thought could not be done. Consequently, the book is designed for a larger audience that would be interested in motivation concepts for everyday issues.

Starting back in the early 1900's, the challenges that I observed or had access to at that time were met with gusto, imagination and a lot of hard work. Some businesses that were started at that time survived many, many years and are talked about to this day. Family ties that were started at that time, and after 100+ years, are continuing to contribute to todays world. The fascinating observation for me is following the genetic trends or patterns of human reactions that may be associated with a particular family or group. The work habits and mind sets of doing innovative things that were evident in the early families are trends that I see in their descendants yet today.

Another example of a trend passed on was the development of a positive attitude that I inherited from watching my family deal with tough farming issues when grain prices were not very good. Polio did impair my walking ability, but it really increased my attitude of finding solutions to overcome challenging conditions and that was a real positive find. It was also my first exposure to people who had the ability to think and try new avenues of creating ways to overcome human health related issues like eliminating full leg braces or monitoring growth in bone tissue. I was fortunate that the doctors that worked with me were innovative thinkers and did try experimental surgery on fusing my ankle to eliminate a full leg brace. It was very successful, and it made me even more intent on finding solutions. The whole polio event had an even bigger response than we imagined at the time. Prior to this time, no one connected to our family had even considered going to college, but it was determined that it was the best avenue for me. Later, many of our family members followed suit.

The fact that I had such a strong family with a good attitude helped me decide to start a family once I found the right girl to marry. Working with other graduate students at Iowa State University helped me meet a great girl from Broomfield, Colorado named Dorothy. It turned out to be a long and rewarding experience. Also, while at graduate school, I ended up doing a graduate program with a professor who was an out-of-the-box thinker.

This was a prime example of trying to find solutions to what seemed like an unrealistic goal. This combined with my childhood quest for finding solutions helped me later in life to developing products that still have not been matched today.

Development of a Business Icon – Denison Candy Kitchen

The beginning of this story begins with my parents, Fritz and Laretta, who were both born in a small rural town in Western Iowa called Denison. The name of the town originated with a Baptist Preacher named Jesse W. Denison. In 1846, Jesse had started an enterprise called Providence Western Land Company with $51,000 from Rhode Island investors. On May 23, 1856, he wrote to the investors that he had found 23,040 acres on the Boyer River where they projected that a railroad would be built. The land office in Council Bluffs considered the registration the next afternoon,

South side of Broadway Montgomery Wards on the corner

Main Street in Denison

and the settlement was then named after Jesse W. Denison. The Denison town site was between the forks of the Boyer River that had been the dividing line between the Sac and Fox Nations and the Sioux.

The first settlers were native born Americans from New England. The first Immigrant group was from Sweden. They bought land north of town for $3 per acre in 1868, that is when the Railroad came to Denison. The next immigration group arrived on August 13, 1870. It consisted of some leading Germans that purchased 520 acres for $6 per acre. Numerous German settlers followed and Crawford County was considered the most fortunate county in the state to establish a German settlement within its borders.

James Bartholomew

One of the establishments that was started in 1903 that had a very long-term effect on the community in terms of popularity and a place to congregate on Saturday night was the Candy Kitchen. The Denison Candy Kitchen started in a small 30 by 40-foot wood frame building by an Italian immigrant, James Bartholomew (originally Gremaldo Bartolomie). James was from Valdo Talvo, Italy, and some townspeople feared him, associating him with the Mafia and the Black Hand. Such was not the case at all as James was a motivated worker. When James was a young boy, he went to England and worked as a busboy at some of the fancy hotels. When WWII broke out, he went back to Italy to serve his time in the army, and then moved to California. From there, he moved to Denison to start a business. James opened it officially on April 11, 1911, the same day that his son Albert was born.

Candy Kitchen started in 1911
James on the right; Bruno (brother-in-law) on the left

Eating and cooking area of the Candy Kitchen later on

Candy Kitchen in early 1980's

In 1913, the opportunity arose for James to move into a building where the Deutsche Opera Hause Gesellschaft was being built, and that was finalized in 1914. At first, the store only sold home-made candies, such as hand dipped chocolates, taffy and hard candies. Once in the new building, hamburgers, sandwiches, chips, fountain cokes, and home-made ice cream became available and was very popular.

Doc   Rich   Jim

The Denison Candy Kitchen was operated by the Bartholomew family until 1936 when Frank Peruzzi became a part owner. It was always a family type affair, James and Mamie Bartholomew and son, Albert, then Frank and his sisters Virginia, Elizabeth, and Mary.

One of the things that had a big impact on the success of the store was the fresh items of ice

Denison Candy Kitchen

Menu

FOUNTAIN MENU

Banana Splits	35¢	Juices, orange, pineapple, or tomato	15¢
Malts & Shakes	25¢	Milk, Coffee or Tea	10¢
Sundaes	25¢	Coca-Cola, Pepsi Cola,	
Sodas	20¢	Root Beer, Orange, Lime,	
Ice Cream, dish	15¢	Lemon or Cherry drinks	10¢
Floats	15¢	Fresh Lemonade and Iced Tea	
Hot Chocolate	15¢	(in season)	
Nuts 5¢ Extra			

SANDWICH MENU

Bacon and Tomato	35¢	Lettuce and Tomato	25¢
Ham and Cheese	35¢	Ham Salad	25¢
Ham and Egg	35¢	Grilled Cheese	25¢
Bacon and Egg	35¢	Fried Egg	20¢
Ham	30¢	Cheese	20¢
Vegetable Hamburger	30¢	Peanut Butter	20¢
Cheeseburger	30¢	Hamburger	20¢
Bar B-Q Hamburger	25¢	Grilled or toasted Sandwiches	
Tuna	25¢	5¢ extra.	

DOUBLE BURGER (1/4 lb. of meat) ..... 35¢

HEINZ

SOUPS .... 25¢		STEWS	
Vegetable - Tomato - Bean - Cream of Chicken - Chicken Rice - Chicken Noodle - Chicken Vegetable - Clam Chowder - Mushroom		Oyster Stew	40¢
		Chicken Stew	40¢
		Beef Stew	40¢
		Chicken Noodle Dinner	40¢
Chili	30¢	Beef Goulash	40¢
		Chop Suey	40¢
Salads	25¢	Beans and Franks	40¢
		Spaghetti & Hot Dogs	40¢
		Macaroni, Macaroni Creole,	
		Spanish Rice or Spaghetti	25¢
		Baked Beans	20¢

— Please pay when served. —

cream products and the candies that were made in the kitchen in the basement and it was only accessible by a hand-operated elevator run by ropes and pulleys. At Christmas time, people would stock up on the fresh home cooked candies that Albert (Bart) and Frank would make downstairs. The smell of anise candy in the wintertime caught everyone's attention. The penny window was a major attraction for young kids looking for all kinds of candy including syrup-filled wax Coke bottles, licorice, gumballs, jawbreakers, taffy, swizzle sticks, tootsie rolls, black cows, bit-o-honey, and slow pokes. Personally, my favorite was the malted milk balls, and I also enjoyed looking at all the comic books and motorcycle magazines. If Frank was busy, and not watching, one could read a little! You just did not want to get caught as he was rather firm on that issue! During the late 1950's when I was in high school, I would also go to the Candy Kitchen at noon break for a hamburger and chocolate malt. At that time it would cost 45¢ for lunch. It was a great menu for the times and the prices were the best around.

During the summertime on a Saturday night, they would bring out the popcorn machine to the sidewalk to sell bags of popcorn. The Candy Kitchen was also connected to the movie theater. When I was a kid, you could get a bag of popcorn for 10¢ and go to a good western movie for 10¢. If you thought it was a very good movie and came back the next night to see it again, it was free.

The Candy Kitchen closed in December of 1983 and it truly represented a business that was successfully run with a family interest. That is a trait that is hard to replace or hire. The family run business program is one that was very common in the seed business as well.

Albert and Virginia Bartholomew were owners and worked at the Candy Kitchen all the time. They did have children during the operation of the Candy Kitchen. They had two boys, Richard and Jim that I interacted with a lot during my school years in the 50's and 60's and am still in contact with them some 60+ years later. There was one daughter, Mary Ann, that was ten years younger than me. They all participated in the business in one way or another during their school years. It was a business to be remembered. All three of their children I would classify as clones of their parents. All were good workers and they looked like they belonged to the Bartholomew family.

The boys and I interacted a lot over the years. We were involved with model airplanes, fishing, go cart racing and motorcycles Jim had a 650 BSA Super Rocket and Rich had a Triumph Bonneville. Jim attracted a lot of attention as he would outrun the police on a gravel road. The police knew where to find Jim's dad, Bart, to tell him that they could not catch him. Jim also enjoyed model airplanes, and we both ended up with Barnstormer stunt planes and a Flying Fool biplane. Jim pursued the airplanes and became a spray pilot.

Early Background of the Strissel Family

Once I started tracing the background of the family history I became hooked on finding out additional information and at this time, there wasn't any document helped to tie all the fractions of information and pictures into a condensed summary. Consequently, I thought it was a great opportunity to capture the information that was still available after 100 plus years and include it in this book.

My dad's parents did involve immigrants from Germany as part of the large settlement in the Denison area. My dad's father was one of six brothers (Louis, Herman Karl, John, Bill, Albert) and two girls (Caroline Marie and Auguste). They were all born between 1881 and 1890. One month after Auguste was born, Herman passed away.

Sometime later, their mother did marry Paul Frank Sydow from Berlin, Germany. An outline of the early Strissel family tree is included in Appendix A.

This turned out to be a very fascinating group and I was able to collect some interesting information and photos. Auguste captured my attention with her style of dressing and especially the hat. I am sure that helped her get the nickname "Gustie". She married Gilbert Mayfield from Plainview, NE and moved to a horse ranch in Lusk, WY. I was able to capture pictures of Gustie, Fritz, and myself on horses at the ranch. They lived on the ranch for several years and eventually moved back to the Sioux City area.

From Left (Lusk, WY)
Lena, Dora, Gustie, Herman, Albert

Top: Louis (left), Herman Karl
Albert, John, Bill

Augusta

Augusta in Lusk, WY

Fritz in Lusk, WY

Two of the Strissel Brothers, Bill and Louis, along with a friend by the name of Charlie Pranski had a Merry Go Round that they would take to county fairs in the summer-time. One event that did get recorded was in 1915 at the Charter Oak County Fair. As you can tell from the picture, it was well attended What was very interesting was how formal the dress attire was for attending a county fair. I thought it was Impressive and different than in later years.

Bill stayed in the Denison area but never married Louis joined the army and was stationed in France. Louis ended up to be a charter member of the Ninus L. Hunt Post 2504 of the VFW. He was the only man to be a continuous member of the Post for 50 years. After the military, he did work in a laboratory in Ames, Iowa and then returned to the Denison area. I did have the opportunity to meet Louis on several occasions and if I would have known then what I know now, I would have had all kinds of questions.

Albert Strissel married Lena Jahn and raised two girls, Adele and Francis. Adele was born in the Charter Oak area, and later married Albert Petersen on March 11, 1939. Adele frequently visited us for numerous parties and dinners until the year 2000 when she passed away at the Denison Care Center. Francis was a foster sister to Adele and married Ben Preis of Ralston, NE.

John Strissel married Katherine Klink and had three children. Albert H. and Roy both lived in California. I did not find any record of where Louise resided.

Caroline Marie Strissel married Frank Krumveida from Preston, Iowa and they raised three children, Frederick Louis, Howard Otto, and Lorane.

Strissel Merry Go Round at the Charter Oak Fair – September 1915

Louis Strissel – 93rd Birthday

Caroline Marie

Adele

Adele and Francis

Herman Karl Ferdinand Strissel was born on 4/28/1885, and on February 22, 1910, he married Dora Muhl. Dora was born in Kostlin, Germany on May 8, 1878. When she was 12 years old, she moved into the Denison area. After their marriage, they resided on a farm that they had purchased 7 miles south of Denison. After 7 years, they sold the farm and moved to Denison where Herman worked as a carpenter.

There was a lot of construction at that time, but I don't know what he worked on. Then, my dad, Fritz, was born on June 22, 1917 in Denison.

In 1933, Herman reclaimed the farm and moved back to the farm and started farming along with Fritz. Initially, a lot of the work was done with horses and that required a lot of hard work and patience. I can remember my dad telling me about one time when he was out cultivating with horses and a storm came up with a lot of lightning and thunder which scared the horses, and they took off on a run across the field.

The farm consisted of a mixture of some real hilly ground along with some good flat areas. Corn was the primary crop at that time along with oats and hay ground. I do remember that corn prices were never good at that time.

In the late 1930's, Fritz stared dating Laretta Arnold, who lived on a farm approximately 4 miles from the Strissel farm. Fritz was also an avid fan of motorcycles at that time. He and Laretta would ride together whenever possible. He started with a Harley, but when Indian came out with something better, he would trade for that.

Fritz   Fritz

Fritz (center) and two friends

Dora and Herman

Fritz and Laretta

Herman Strissel

Corn Planter

Early Background of the Arnold Family

My mother, Laretta Sophia Marie Strissel, was born July 5, 1923, the daughter of Fred and Ella Haase Arnold. Laretta was born on the Arnold family farm approximately 8 miles south of Denison and 4 miles southwest of the Strissel family farm. The farm consisted of 160 acres that also included a farmhouse and several other buildings. Over the years, several people were born inside the farmhouse. Laretta's dad was born there and to keep him warm during cold spells, they would place the baby bed on the lid of the oven. A total of three brothers and three daughters were born there. Laretta spent some time on the oven lid, but her brother Elmer, was born on Christmas Day so he spent more time there than Laretta.

When Laretta was two years old, they had a big Christmas tree with candles on it. She got too close and it caught on fire. They never had much of a tree after that, in fact, it was limited to a small tree on the table. She never got scolded by her dad for that or anything else according to the information that I received.

Laretta went to a country school that was one mile north of the farm and they usually walked if the weather was good. When they walked home and there was smoke coming out of the chimney, they knew their mom was in a good mood. If there was no smoke, even in the summer they knew she was not feeling good. They cooked everything on the stove.

Arnold Farm-1900

Herman and Sophia Haase
Ella's Parents

John Fredrick and Ella Haase
Arnold (Laretta's Parents)

Laretta

Laretta and Elmer

Laretta

21

During the summer, they had a super large garden, a large grape patch and a huge pumpkin patch. The pumpkins were fed to the hogs and they ate them like they were candy. Every day, Laretta would also feed the hogs ear corn. Then, every couple of weeks she would go collect the cobs. There was always manure on the cobs so she would hit them together to eliminate some of the excess and then take them to the house where they were used in the cook stove or a pot belly stove for heat. Recycling had already begun in the early 1900's!

In addition to the garden work and feeding the pumpkins to the hogs, there were always the chickens, ducks and geese to feed. She also had to take time to manage the care of the dolls and her best four-legged friend! I am sure helping with the laundry worked into the scene on numerous occasions.

Laretta

Laretta

Laretta

Laretta

Laretta and Fred (Her Dad)

I don't know if she had anything to do with the horses, but they were used to harvest the field corn by hand. The wagons were always set up with a bang board on one side so you did not throw the ears over the wagon. Managing work horses and hand-picking corn are two tough jobs and it takes a lot of time. The harvested ear corn would be placed in corn cribs for storage and would be shelled later or be fed directly to the livestock. All of these projects required extra help and this is where having good neighbors helped tremendously.

Hand picking corn with horses   Wagon load of picked corn

Unloading picked corn

In addition to having access to good neighbors, there were also strong family ties that typically meant that everyone had a part in helping with some part of the farming operation. It was apparent from the number of pictures found, that Grandpa and Grandma Hasse spent time with Laretta, and that was another part of the strong family ties.

Laretta (4 years old)   Mr. and Mrs. Herman Haase, Ella, Laretta, Elmer 1928

Laretta and her Dad (Fred)   Jean, Edward,
                                              Allan Valerie, Neila

Laretta worked on the family farm until November 12, 1939, when she was united in marriage to Fritz Strissel at the Zion Lutheran Church by Reverend C.W. Schmidt. They started their new life on the Strissel farm where Fritz had been helping his parents since 1933.

Laretta's brother, Elmer, was born on December 24, 1918. On January 5, 1941, he married Phyliss McBride. They resided on farms in the Buck Grove and Deloit vicinities until 1954 when they moved to Denison. Elmer worked as a carpenter and for the Coca Cola Co and for the J&O Oil Company. The last eight years of his life he worked as a line-man for the Denison Municipal Utilities. They had six children,

Friedrick who died in infancy, Jean, Edward, Allen, Neila, and Merlin. Over the years, they would come out for birthday parties and we would go to their house to play board games and softball in a vacant lot next to their house.

Marriage of Fritz Strissel and Laretta Arnold

O n the day of their wedding, they were harvesting corn on the home place that later became known as the forty. At noon, they had a goose dinner that was attended by Fritz's folks (Herman and Dora), Elmer, Phyllis, Laretta, and her mom, Ella. Laretta's dad had passed away the previous year.

After dinner, Fritz, Laretta, Elmer and Phyllis went to Rev. Schmitz's house to get married. They then went to Cronk's café and had chocolate malts and then to someone's house for pictures. Ella did not inform Herman of the wedding until after they left for the wedding. When they came home later that afternoon, they continued harvesting the corn until it was finished. After harvest, Ella packed them goose sandwiches and they took off for California for their honeymoon.

Fritz and Laretta

Fritz and Laretta

Fritz and Laretta

Laretta   Laretta   Fritz and Laretta

Fritz at the farm   1939 Allis Chalmers

1941 Farmall H

When they returned from California, they moved to the Strissel Farm where Fritz had been farming my himself since 1938 when his folks moved back to Denison. Fritz paid them $500.00 per year until they died. Dad's mother passed away on 7/3/1942 and Herman passed on 11/23/1945. Ella moved to a house in Denison in 1942 and lived there until she passed away on 6/14/1966.

The Strissel family farm consisted of 200 acres with a mix of some bottom ground and several steep hills. When they first started, they did use horses, and they would pick corn by hand. I can remember my dad telling me of cultivating corn with the horses, and a storm came up and the thunder scared the horses so much that they just headed across the field running back to the barn. It was physically impossible to stop them. One year later they purchased a 1939 Allis Chalmers to do the field work. Then they could cultivate with the tractor, and they purchased a two-row corn picker for the tractor. Two years later they purchased a 1941 Farmall tractor. Later, they purchased a 1956 Allis Chalmers that had extra power for a lot of the field work.

Early Childhood Days of the Strissel Children

In March of 1942, their world just took on a new phase as I and my twin sister, Judith, entered the world. Therein, the story behind "What's Up Doc" begins. Unfortunately, Judith had an open spine at birth and was unable to be a part of the ongoing story. Two years later, another sister, Janet, was born, but she also had health problems and only lived 8 months. Then, in 1946, my brother Daniel entered the world and got a lot of attention as he was a cute little fella!

Fritz, Jerry, Judith, Laretta

Dan & Fritz

Jerry & Dan

Dan & Laretta

Jerry on Main Street in Denison

Jerry and Offenhauser race car

Grandpa Herman and Jerry

Start of Jerry's aviation hobby

Life on the farm for us in the early years was quite simple as there was very little interaction with the outside world. Activities included collecting eggs, helping with dishes, processing chickens, riding scooters or bikes, sneaking out of naps in the afternoon, playing cards or board games and exploring the creeks for fish, turtles, or frogs. TV was available at one point, but there was only 3 Omaha channels that could be watched. Consequently, Saturdays were fun as shows like Sky King, Lassie, cartoons and westerns could fill your time slot in the morning. Sundays typically consisted of going to church followed by a big meal at noon. Roast beef with potatoes, onions, and carrots or fried chicken with baked potatoes were usually the choices.

In the early years, dad also had milk cows, laying hens, Hereford cattle, feeder pigs and broiler chickens. They typically raised 100 chickens to butcher for the family. Everyone participated in this event. My mother was a master at frying the chicken and especially the gizzards. I have tried many times to match it myself, but so far, not successful.

Jerry's favorite ride

New sheriff in control
of the chickens

Jerry's first contest

Angel Food Cake made from scratch

Dan and Judy Meyer

Birthday parties were always fun as we would have the neighbor kids over plus our cousins. Grandma Ella would occasionally attend also. We would usually have an angel food cake along with ice cream as it was always a big hit. The birthday must be from Dan's party since I usually had a snowstorm on my birthday.

One of my favorite hobbies starting at this early age was flying model airplanes. I even competed in a contest that they had at the Denison Airport when I was quite young. That was the start of a hobby that now has carried on for over 70 years. At this time, most of the airplane flying was done using thin cables that were 50-60' long depending on the size of the plane and they were flown in a circle. My dad would build larger models that I would eventually fly also. One of the most interesting events that occurred during this early time is that a lot of the larger engines originally had a point and condenser system like a car along with a Champion spark plug, however, people learned how to remove all of that and convert it to a glow plug system that was much easier to use. I still have some of the original motors that were used that had the points and condenser along with a system where you could retard the spark. In fact, I have some from that era have never been run and are in new condition.

Having animals on the farm in those days was a must. Dan and I started off with a collie, and then after a period, my dad started raising Alaskan Huskies that were pure white, large and very strong. We did generate some pups that we sold, and we did keep one male that we named Nicki who was gorgeous. One day, the father, King, and Nicki got into one fierce battle that was a determining factor in deciding that maybe we should incorporate a new breed on the farm. The next dog was a Keeshond named Rocky, and this was way before the movie came out which is good because this Rocky was a lover not a fighter.

Dan, Lassie, Jerry   Huskies – King, Susie, and Nicki

Vicki and Rocky   Vicki, Rocky and Grandpa

One of the big items on the farm was to raise pigs not only for sale, but also for taking them to a local butcher to for us to process. There usually was an intense discussion on whether we got the right meat back. Raising pigs was rather labor intense and getting them to go in the right place always seemed to be a challenge. It was very common for pigs to find an opening by which to escape and getting them back into the yard was always a fun experience. Raising Duroc pigs was my favorite and riding them when they were big was quite exciting! If they call riding lambs mutton busting, then this was pork chop busting.

Feeder pigs   Duroc hogs

One of the favorite activities for the farm kids was playing board games or playing cards. I always thought that playing cards had a positive effect on one learning math in school. No hard evidence to prove that, but I did have more than one person think the same thing. It was very common for the neighbors or friends from town to come out to play cards during the week. They played a variety of poker games along with Buck Yuker and Pitch. If Grandma Ella came out, they would play canasta. When the neighbors came over to play cards, the kids would always play in the other room or outside. It was a well-known tradition that my mother would always have sandwiches or cookies or bars for these events. As we got older, we did get to join in on the games and we had a lot of fun.

The neighbors also played a key role in helping with shelling corn from the corn crib. This was a major project as all the corn that was picked at that time was ear corn One of the side attractions to this project was that it would scare out the large rats from the corn crib and the dogs would catch them and shake them like crazy. This was a completely natural reaction as they were never trained for this and every dog would do the same thing.

Another neighborhood event was the baling of hay and then placing it in the barn. This involved collecting the bales on a hay rack, taking it to the barn, staking 8 or 9 in a pile that was then placed in the grips of a large fork. then with a tractor, they would pull the stack into the barn, trip it to unload it and then someone in the barn would stack them. This was another labor-intensive event that took a lot of time and usually during hot weather. Again, my mother would make sure they had something to eat and drink.

There was another major undertaking that occurred before I was born, but I was intrigued by it as it did involve a lot of hard labor and it was the creation of a basement under our existing farmhouse. I do not know all the individuals involved, but I did recognize Paul Craig in the photograph that I found.

Paul and his wife Mildred lived approximately 3 miles from our farm. Years later, I became good friends with them and I helped Paul with several projects and we played a lot of cards, watched football games and played a lot of snooker. They had a 1951 Pontiac, but could not drive anymore, so I was their personal driver on some occasions.

Strissel farmhouse   Paul Craig (middle)

One of our neighbors was Donna Mullenger who later became known as Donna Reed. She made some great movies like "From Here to Eternity", It's a Wonderful Life", and basically made Denison well known. The city conducted many annual celebrations in honor of Donna Reed with a parade and several acting classes. Most of the main characters in the TV series or the movies participated in the event. One of the highlights for my dad was that he gave Donna Reed a ride on his Harley Davidson.

Mullenger Family   Doma Reed

Donnabelle Mullenger was of German decent, born in Denson on January 27, 1921. There were so many Germans in Denison that they decided that there should be a large opera house. In 1914, the 775-seat Deutsche Opernhaus Gesellschaft von Denison was built at the corner of Main and Broadway. This building would later house the museum named after Donna Reed.

Donna Reeds' sister, Karen, was in the same grade as me in the Denison school system. I will always remember her dad, Bill, who drove a white Cadillac out to their farm every year to plant a tree. They were a very nice family.

When I look back at this time of my life, I seriously cannot remember any time when we just sat in a chair and made the comment "I'm bored". I would guess that due to our culture, we just found something fun to do or we were in an environment where there was always something that needed to be done. Up until writing this piece, I always would get irritated when I heard kids saying that, but you know, the new social media has created this new trend that would promote that type of reaction.

It was at this point where I really started thinking about comparing my early childhood with today's childhood environment. Not many writers would compare corn genetics to human genetics, but I have a perception that I would like to share. When a corn breeder starts to develop new material, they usually start with an open pollinated population of corn. This population typically consists of corn plants that have different plant heights, big ears, small ears, some plants with good stalks and other plants with poor stalks. A breeder starts to isolate all the plants with good traits. After 5-6 years of selection, they finally develop lines of corn that have an accumulation of yield genes, disease resistance, and overall good health. Working with other plant breeders throughout the world, one creates genetic diversity in the corn world. Then a good manager will place that material with an end-user or grower that can make the most of it.

The human population is also very diverse, and over time, with the help of social media, sources of information has become readily available to many young people. When I observe young kids today, I see a string of young minds that have accumulated all sorts of information and they have tremendous potential. I don't think they realize that at this stage, but it is there. At this point, adults can play an important role in exposing their hidden talents. I know in my seed foundation company I have hired young people who have talents that can benefit the operation of the company in many ways. Surrounding yourself with good people is a real benefit. Overall, information from people all over the world has helped accumulate valuable information for medicine, corn genetics, space exploration, health benefit electronics, just to name a few.

Polio

In 1951, everyday life at the farm changed forever. Dan and I were some of the first people in the area to contract polio. On October 8, 1951, Dan came home from school with a bad headache. They went to the county hospital where they determined it was polio, and they sent him to the St. Joseph Hospital in Sioux City, Iowa. Paralysis of both legs and his right arm set in almost immediately. Four days later, I could not put my right leg down and it hurt. Consequently, I was taken to the hospital and I was diagnosed with Polio also. I was also transferred to Sioux City. Paralysis of my left leg set in right away. There are certain events that I remember very well at the hospital. The first thing that I will not forget is being wrapped in hot cloth for the first three days. The next event was putting me on a canvas connected to a hoist that lowered you into a big tank of water. It was quite an experience for this young farm boy. The other thing that I will never forget is seeing all the kids in iron lungs in the hallways as all the rooms were filled. They let us go home over Christmas. We were allowed to go home, and this is when the newspaper did an article on us concerning the encounter with Polio.

At the time of this article, neither one of us could walk. Our shoes had a board attached to the heels of both shoes to keep our feet and legs straight. I could crawl everywhere, but mom had to carry Dan. We did go back for more rehab, and in total the process took about three months. Our mom stayed with us almost all the time. At the end, Dan had his legs recover enough to walk, but his right arm remained totally paralyzed. I ended up with my left leg totally paralyzed and was fitted with a full leg brace. Soon after this, it was determined that my right leg was growing much faster than my left leg. When there was ¾ "difference in length, the doctors decided that they would put three staples on both sides of my right knee to slow down the growth so that I would not end up with a huge difference. It worked, but I ended up to be 5'6" instead of the predicted 5'10".

During this whole process, we went to two doctors, Dr. Donahue and Dr. O'Donahue, in Sioux City. I remember one meeting with them that I would never forget. They wanted to try an experimental surgery that would eliminate the use of the bulky leg brace. They wanted to fuse my ankle at an angle by transferring bone. To me at the time, this was just awful news. I was one of the fastest runners at school and this just eliminated any possibility I thought I might have of getting back to normal. As a kid, I did not really understand that it was permanent nerve damage. We did the surgery and I was in a cast for three months during the summer. It was a long three months as it was either hurting or itching. In the end, and to this day, it was very successful and I am thankful that these doctors were out-of-the-box thinkers. For some reason, I continued to encounter individuals throughout my life that had that capability and I firmly think it influenced a lot of my decisions in career decisions. One prime example is my decision to extract the protein out of white corn and replace all the fish meal in fish farming that eliminates all the bad contaminants in the fish humans eat.

My brother Dan also maintained a positive attitude during the polio event and he has kept it to this day. Playing cards, model trains, Christmas trees and decorations, and boating were some of his favorite things that kept him entertained. He also spent a lot of time with mom and became an expert on following the family tree and other neighborhood interactions. I think he has a computer chip in his head as he has an endless memory bank that I tapped a lot for the information in this book. We were also great fans of going to town on Saturday night and going to the movies. The best part was that the Candy Kitchen was directly attached to the theater and you could get popcorn and the best malted milk balls around.

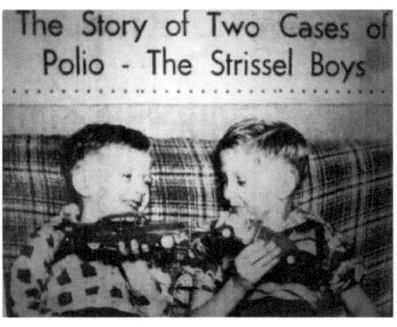
The Story of Two Cases of Polio - The Strissel Boys

I did find out years later that the doctors had given the folks some advice for moving forward. They basically told them to treat us as normal kids that needed to go to school, do chores, and let them figure out how to do things. It turned out to be excellent advice for us!

Following rehab at the hospital, Dan and I proceeded with life participating in the farm activities and going to school. Naturally, we could not do a lot of things at the time, but it was amazing what we ended up doing. Life on the farm was rather straight forward, simple, and creating fun things to do was the key. There were a lot of good farm ponds and lakes around where we could also do some fishing. This was also an excuse to go play in the creeks to catch minnows.

Shortly after rehab I did have several surgeries to keep my leg straight and to keep the good leg from growing too much faster than the affected left leg. Basically, they inserted three staples on both sides of my right knee. This meant that my height ended up to be 5'6" instead of 5'10".

The last surgery happened when I was in fourth grade and it kept me from any recess activity. However, I did have a very good friend, Louis Poggensee, who stayed with me to play cards during the recess time. After recovery, we would play endless games of marbles during recess or at noon breaks. This was one of those examples of a true friendship and it stayed that way forever. In later times, Louis became a God Father to my daughter, Vicki, and I was the best man at his wedding.

Fortunately, my dad was interested in building and flying model airplanes. The opportunity to build planes from kits was great for me as additional surgeries provided extra down time for me to build. Once I got started, I was destined to do it to this day. I still remember going to the five and dime store in town and buying a new kit for 85¢. At that time, we would build control line planes that we would fly with 60' wires. This required a large area that had to be mowed with a push mower. It would take about two hours to get it ready. My dad was quite good at flying these planes being able to do all kinds of stunts. Naturally, I proceeded with learning the stunts as well. The best part of this hobby was that I found it really rewarding to see a finished product, and basically, it was something you could do without thinking about what you could not do under my existing condition of leg paralysis. I found this hobby so interesting that I went into aeronautical engineering at Iowa State University. I did not continue with that major, but I did continue with building and flying model airplanes.

Biplane with an Atwood 60 Engine   Dan and Laretta

Jerry and Dan   Homemade boat and a 1955 Oldsmobile

Development of a Positive Attitude

Later, in my teenage years, I took a major step in persuing opportunities that I previously thought were not physically possible. A friend was out visiting the farm one day and he had a 500 single cylinder BSA motorcycle. I got the opportunity to try and ride it. I had no trouble handling it and from then on I traveled the countryside

500 Single Cylinder BSA

on a motorcycle. We went to the Sturgis motorcycle rally 23 years in a row, dirt track races in Dodge City, Kansas, Springfield, Missouri, Elkhorn, Wisconsin, Columbus, Ohio, hill climbs, and a road race in Indianapolis, Indiana.

Looking back, I find it amazing how that one event had such a positive and motivating effect on my life. This could be one of the reasons that I created this positive attitude and am always looking for solutions instead of throwing in the towel. In addition to traveling on a motorcycle, I also raced go-carts, went bowling, drove tractors, and even had the nerve to date girls. I did take Carol Ridgley to a junior high dance although I don't think I mastered the art of dancing. I also had girlfriends that liked to ride motorcycles and some even attended the races at Dodge City, Kansas, and Sturgis, South Dakota.

Jerry and Carol junior high   Jerry – 1960 BSA

Jerry and Candi   Elaine, In Norton, Kansas

Jerry and Nancy senior prom   Jerry - Sturgis

I would have to say that my dad was one of those individuals who always approached a challenge or a new project with a positive and fun attitude. He built his own boat learning how to apply fiberglass along with adding colors. He also built his own skies and a surfboard that we had a lot of fun with. Other fascinating solutions included changing the gear shifting from the left side of the BSA motorcycle to the right side. Also, the original carburetor did not perform the best, so he found another type, inserted it, and it worked great.

Friends Forever

Overall, my parents were both hard working, fun-orientated people who enjoyed doing activities with other people. I would also have to say they were both fascinating and classy people of that time period. I don't ever remember them having a real negative attitude. There were a lot of tough and challenging issues, but they always looked for a solution. I am confident that trait along with the people-orientated characteristic was also carried over to Dan and me. It is a trait that I think can be one of the most powerful tools to overcome tough challenges. My mother had severe asthma and would get terrible coughing attacks, but she would take a treatment and come back in the room with a smile and ready to play cards.

My dad and I did a lot of fishing in Canada on the Winnipeg River, and we did take several different people with us on several occasions. Keith "Tex" McCoid went with us once and it created a story that my dad never forgot. We had gone seven miles up river and back into a bay area that was good for Northern Pike. It was in the spring and the females were spawning in these areas. There were a lot of tree stumps in this bay, so we went to the shore so we could walk back in the bay to do some casting. On the way back we saw a lot of bear droppings but did not see any bears. I had been casting for about 20 minutes when I heard a distinct rustling in the bushes. My immediate thought was it was a bear, I threw my favorite rod and reel down and took off. My dad was watching this and suddenly, a big rabbit and not a bear came out of the bushes, There was a lot of laughing and kidding that following that event.

Another fun event happened in Canada when Albert "Bart" Bartholomew went with us to go fishing. When we were there, we became friends with a local resident and he invited us over for some of his home-brewed beverages. Bart was not a lover of beer, but he was a good sport and sampled everything. The next morning my dad oversaw making pancakes and he used beer in the batter without telling Bart. The pancakes turned light and fluffy, but when Bart put syrup on his pancakes, he suddenly made a loud statement claiming that they tasted just like the beverages we had the night before they had the taste of a strong beer. We had a fun time with it, and Bart was just fascinated with the fact that you could not taste it until you put syrup on the pancake.

Dad's homemade boat

Tex and Jerry in bear country

Fritz and Jerry, Canada

Tex and Jerry, Canada

Future fishing trips included going to Leach Lake in Minnesota fishing for walleyes, going to farm ponds for bass, Marble Lake for bullheads and then to the Fort Randle Dam in South Dakota to snag for paddle fish in the Missouri River. The largest one I caught was 45 pounds and it was a thrill for me. Dad had converted an old refrigerator to a smoke house, and he would smoke the fish for several days. They were exceptionally good tasting, and they do not have any bones, just cartilage.

Another fun activity was being avid motorcycle enthusiasts. We enjoyed riding and for going to half-mile dirt track racing, mile dirt track racing, short track racing, and hill climbs. The Sturgis Rally in South Dakota was one of our favorite places as it had every thing. The fun part of the event was meeting people from all over the country and seeing some of their modified bikes. One year, we had 23 bikers in our group and that was a lot of fun. One trip event I will always remember is when my dad and I were traveling with other bikers and we stopped at a rest stop in South Dakota. We ended up talking to a family on vacation, and it turned out that they first thought we belonged to a bad gang of motorcyclists. We laughed about that all the way to Sturgis as our group was mainly a bunch of farmers.

Fritz and Jerry - 45# paddle fish   Hill Climb in Denison – 1930's

One year, my dad and I rode a 1960 BSA out to Columbus, Ohio for a professional half-mile race. The total trip cost us $8.37 for gas. On the way back, we did encounter one scary moment on a two-lane highway that had a bunch of little hills. I happened to be the one driving, and I came over the top of one of the hills to find a bunch of 40-pound feeder pigs crossing the highway. Amazingly,, I went right through the middle of the pack without hitting one. That could have been a real problem.

Genetic Inheritance of Human Traits

There is a fascinating side story to my relationship with the Bartholomew boys, especially Jim, and it involves genetic inheritance of traits outside of corn genetics. When we were growing up and doing all the outdoor activities together, one would typically classify Rich and myself as conservative whereas Jim was much more daring and prone to taking risks that typically involved crashes. For example, one day Jim got a

Jim's 1951 Chevy

little carried away on a curvy gravel country road south of Denison and ended up putting his car on top of a fence post. Jim did survive the crash with some head wounds that caused a lot of bleeding. Instead of going to the hospital, he went to see his dads' brother, Reynold, to get his help and advice before checking in with dad. Reynold was a mild-mannered man who fit in with our group as he also rode motorcycles. In fact, the newspaper did publish a picture of him with his wife, Freida, as the newly-weds rode away on their Indian motorcycle. Their attire in the pictures were very typical of the times, especially for motorcycle riders.

At first, I classified myself and Rich as conservative, but then I remembered that Rich did roll Tony Clark's dad's car on the north side of Denison. Rich and Tony were thrown out of the car and Rich broke his arm. I also remembered that I did have two separate accidents where I hit a car with my 1960 BSA bending the front forks back against the motor. This was on a 4-lane highway right in Denison. I flew over the car landing in the opposite lane with no injuries. We did get the forks straightened out and the following week, dad and I headed to Dodge City, Kansas for a motorcycle race. The following year I had a car pull out in front of me in Lake View, Iowa, and again the front forks ended up against the motor and I ended on top of the hood of the car without any injuries. Later in my life, I had another motorcycle accident that I will cover later. Jumping ahead, I will say that it turns out that my middle daughter, Vicki, has been nicknamed "Crash" for several reasons and she maybe inherited certain traits from dad. There are several other features that she has that truly resemble how good old dad would respond to certain situations.

The story of genetic inheritance of traits from the parents will continue to build as I proceed with the story of Jim.

| Reynold Bartholomew | Freida | Reynold and Freida Just Married! |

After high school, Jim enlisted in the military in 1966 and ended up in the 355th Tactical Fighters division and was stationed in Thailand as a jet engine mechanic working on the F105 fighter planes. His brother Rich was drafted into the Army and was stationed in Germany. After returning from the military, Jim married Doris Plagge. He continued his interest in aviation by managing the Devision Municipal Airport and later the Airport in Storm Lake, IA. He also started a crop spraying service as the demand for the spraying of crops for insects and diseases really increased over time.

Prior to writing this book, I had the opportunity to sit down with Jim to discuss his adventures concerning the art of crop spraying. As one can imagine, crop spraying is not for the timid or hobby flyer as it is risky flying low over fields and between telephone wires and fences. In addition, they are applying fungicides and other chemicals that must be handled with care. Typically, once the crop spraying season begins, there are a lot of hours put in with a limited amount of sleep. Then if you are flying on a hot day with the sun beating down on the canopy, one must really concentrate on staying awake. There is not much room for errors, and in 1976, Jim crashed his Pawnee spray plane. I do not know how he survived, but he did although it was tough on his body. In 1984, he crashed his Piper Brave and he survived that one also. And now for the rest of the story on genetic Inheritance.

Crop Spraying

Jim and Doc

Pawnee Spray Plane

Pawnee Spray Plane

Jim's Spray Plane

Jim has two sons, John and Mike, that have taken up the art of crop spraying and helping at the Storm Lake Airport. Jim has his own hanger where he keeps all his spray planes and his personal collection of planes like his restored Stearman PT17.

Jim's son, Mike, followed his dad's footsteps in that he also had a crash with his spray plane, and again, it was a miracle that he survived, and in this case, Mike only got a cut on his right wrist. If you look at the photo close, you will see the bandage on his right arm above his wrist. I had indications from Jim that he had a lot of other traits that were very similar to Dad. As Jim would say, "He is a chip off the old block!"

Jim's Harley Hummer   Mike Bartholomew – 401 Air Tracker

Mike   Jim's hanger – Air Tracker

Jim's restored Stearman PT17   Jim Bartholomew, Jerry &
                                    Dorothy Strissel

Jim also had restored the 1961 BSA Super Rocket that he used to escape from the police many years ago. Unfortunately, it is also an example of how both of us have kept our special projects and have now realized that we cannot use them like we use to due to physical limitations. They are still fun to have, but the eventual decision of what to do with them is a challenging question. The one bike that he wishes that he should have kept is an old Harley Davidson Hummer that we basically restored from the frame up. Today it would be worth a lot of money.

College

A new adventure was in store for me after graduating from high school. I don't remember discussing it at the time, but I think the folks were convinced that due to my disability from polio, I should go to college and learn a new business other than farming. Since I had such an interest in airplanes, I decided to go to Iowa State University and major in aeronautical engineering. I also joined a fraternity my first year. Both events were way out of the norm for this farm boy. In fact, I don't remember visiting any college before applying for acceptance. I was the first of our families to go to college and it encouraged other members of our extended family to go to college or a trade school. Young people today have access to all kinds of information concerning advanced learning opportunities in colleges or trade schools, In fact, my 10-year-old granddaughter, Pyper, has already been to several clinics at Iowa State University and has performed at half-time at basketball and football games.

When I was asked to pledge at the fraternity, I did not know any of the members or the other pledges. It was an exciting time as I met people from all over the world. Two of the young men I met turned out to be best friends forever. Herm was from Oxford, Connecticut and Ray was from Closter, New Jersey, 10 miles from New York City. They were from two areas that I was not familiar with at all at that time. It was a very diverse group of young men, and they all had different backgrounds that contributed to some very interesting conversations. I learned many new things during my first year.

All of us new pledges got hassled, but it did build relationships and teamwork for us. It was also an opportunity to learn some useful information from the upper classmen in what to expect from a lot of the coarse work. The house mother was an exceptional person who was well suited to manage a wild group of young men. One of the main items I learned was manners at the dinner table and it was something I never forgot. It cost a nickel for every mistake, so after one week, one tended to learn very quickly. It was also my first experience in sleeping in an open window room with a multitude of other men. It was rather cool during the winter and I would not want to do it for the rest of my life.

Participation in a fraternity was a means to social events that involved introduction to drinking, dance parties, girls and sports. It was a learning experience, but it was also very time consuming and even though the fraternity stressed studying, it was difficult to manage the right amount of time to get the best grades. At the end of the first year, Ray, Herman and I left the fraternity to concentrate on our education. We were fortunate to find an English professor who wanted to rent the back half of his house that had a private entrance. This turned out to be an ideal location for us as it was close to campus. The three of us all went to the same church that was on campus and focused on college students. It did promote social events and I must admit that it was my first exposure to pizza. Talk about living in an isolated world prior to college, it was hard for my roommates to believe this one.

At the close of the first year, I met with my councilor to review my agenda in aeronautical engineering. During the school year, and specifically college physics classes, I met some students that were quite advanced in their ability to solve problems. I think it was my first exposure to that kind of talent. I enjoyed designing projects like a truss for an airplane hanger, but I was concerned about what exactly most of the graduates did after graduation. I met with my counselor, and the picture he painted was not what I was expecting. In his mind, he was projecting working in a closed environment with 50 other engineers competing against one another. Based on my background of growing up on a farm and doing all kinds of outdoor activities, I decided to change my major to botany with the idea of going into teaching biology in high school. Apparently, the love of interacting with people helped in making this decision that did follow me in all my future endeavors.

We had a great character-building time during our college career that turned into a lasting friendship. Both Ray and Herm spent several holidays with me at the family farm in Denison, Iowa. As expected, my folks thoroughly enjoyed them being there and they got to hear many good stories of activities on the east coast. Ray's home in New Jersey was only 10 miles from New York city and he was accustomed to all the busy activities of the city, He would tell me that we were just existing out here in the mid-west. Ray's dad was a plumber, and he had encountered some fascinating events over the years. It did not take Ray too long before he really enjoyed being in the Midwest area. In fact, he ended up living in the Midwest after graduation. Life is depended upon what you make of it. Herman's parents ran a dog kennel, and they kept dogs for many people including the owners of Dupont. Herm was very good around the dogs we had at the farm and his plans were to go to the vet college at Iowa State. Herman was also a proud participant in the Drum and Bugle Core in New Jersey. We were not familiar with all the hard work they put into this activity, but we learned a lot from Herm during his visit.

Herman in Oxford, CT   Ray and his 1957 Ford

During an Easter break, my mother decided to turn Herman loose on planting potatoes on Good Friday. Without her knowing, he very carefully cut out all the eyes of the potatoes and planted them with the sprout just sticking out of the ground. She was totally shocked when he showed her his work! They were placed very evenly in a nice row, and she knew he spent a lot of time on it. They did grow, but she never forgot that project. She mentioned it every time we talked about our favorite visitors.

When we first moved into our new house of residence, I was surprised when Ray introduced me to his country music collection. For some reason, I was not expecting that from someone not known as a country boy, but Ray was a big country music fan like me and every year the three of us would go to the Johnny Cash show at the KRNT theater in Des Moines. It was a great show as there would be additional singer like the Statler Brothers, Conway Twitty and of course, June Carter. We went to this event whenever we had a chance. When I look back at these years, I still find it fascinating that we had such a fun relationship that developed between individuals from completely different backgrounds.

The true test of being good friends was when we started pulling franks on one another. One example happened when Herm was on a date. Ray had a fancy white 1957 Ford car with black fender skirts that he would let us use for dates. One night, Herm had a date and while they were in the movie, we removed the skirts and put them in the trunk. When Herm came out of the movie and saw that, he immediately called the police. After they were there for a few minutes, they suggested looking in the trunk. We had a good laugh, but Herm did not quite see it that way at the time. He was a good sport and would eventually get even with us.

Summer breaks during undergraduate school meant Ray and Herm would be going back to the East Coast. I went back to help at the farm and earn extra money doing odd jobs. It was always a great time as it meant boating at Lake View, fishing, playing snooker, racing go-carts, riding motorcycles, raising and selling sweetcorn, going to professional motorcycle hill climbs, the Springfield Mile motorcycle race in Illinois, half-mile motorcycle racing in Dodge City, Kansas, and going to the annual motorcycle rally in Sturgis South Dakota.

South Dakota was a special event in that usually we had a lot of friends riding along with us for a week of meeting people from all over the world. One year, we did have 23 people join us in riding out to Sturgis. During the event, main street was closed so that only motorcycles could park on it. That also meant that it was a great opportunity to view all the different bikes We did spend time with some farmers from Almena, Kansas who came there after putting up hay, and they just wanted to visit and meet people.

We started out sleeping in a pup tent at this event, but after getting soaked from heavy rains a couple of times, we decided to rent a motel room on a year-to-year basis. It was a very basic, and inexpensive but was nice and over the years we met some very interesting people. I will never forget one year there were some union workers from Indiana there that were on strike. It was my first exposure to that group and I quickly found out that they were not going to try and find any other work to make ends meet. That was a completely different mind set that this country boy was not used to at that time. I never forgot that conversation as it did make me aware of a whole different set of standards for large corporations and their work force.

Another year, we met some riders from Minnesota that were staying at the same motel and one guy was called Pappa Smurf, as he did work as Santa Claus in Minneapolis. Great people, however, early one morning I got up and went outside to see the group gathered at the picnic table having a beer and teaching my daughter Vicki how to carve her name in the table.

Fortunately, their table was meant to be autographed as dictated by the times. We did not promote that type of activity, but it did provide us with some interesting stories to tell over the years that followed. We were also fortunate to meet many racers that would either race in the short track races or the half-mile event. Both types were fun to watch, but at the short track event you could sit right next to the corner where a lot of action occurred. At the end of the night, you would be covered with red dirt.

I did learn another valuable lesson in watching and talking to these young racers. One might think you are good at handling a motorcycle, but once you see some of these young men riding side by side and throwing the bike into a slide at speeds up to 130-140 mph on a mile dirt track, you know that takes a special talent.

A key for me was identifying talent in the corn genetic and marketing world and utilizing it in a manner that was beneficial to everyone. The old saying that one way of being successful in business is to surround yourself with good people is very true! The Sturgis Rally was one of those events that we continued going to for 23 years in a row. It was one of those times where one just took time to have some fun, and we never regretted it.

Neil Keen on the ½ mile track

There were several friends that not only participated in our travels to the Sturgis Rally but had a working or a fun-type relationship throughout the year with us. Ron Schimmer and his wife, Jackie, were prime examples as they went to Sturgis with us but would also deliver fuel to our farm. Their sons, Mike and Shane, became avid motorcycle enthusiasts, and their daughter, Michele participated in our other family functions. Bob Boeck and his son Charles, farmed approximately 3 miles from our farm and were avid motorcycle fans also. Charles and I traveled together to several races on our cycles including Sturgis. I also did some work for Paul and Marcia Losh who were in the construction business, but also big motorcycle fans. Bill Miller, a superintendent at the Manilla School System, and his wife Marylin would also join us on cycle events. There were many other friends as well, but the key point here was that when anybody needed help with a project (or illness) any of these people were willing to help.

I must mention another lesson learned during the summer months and it was connected to my model airplane endeavors. Another student at Iowa State also had an interest in flying model airplanes and we decided to compete in a control line stunt contest in Des Moines, Iowa. The airplane I was using for the contest had an antique motor that my dad had. It was an old Atwood 60 motor that originally had a point and ignition system with a Champion spark plug just like a car, but he had removed the point system and converted it to a glow plug type engine. At any rate, I crashed the plane doing one of the stunt maneuvers and I broke the needle valve on the motor. I had now created a problem in that these antique motors were no longer being made and you could not get parts for them. It was at this time that I became aware of a gentlemen in Des Moines that was a collector of antique model airplane engines. I now discovered a whole new network of antique engine collectors. I had no idea that this existed

Atwood 60

and now I not only got a needle valve for my Atwood engine, but I was able to buy brand new model airplane antique engines. I did buy some brand-new Atwood 60 motors with the original ignition system and the Champion spark plug. In addition, I did buy a new Anderson Spitfire 60 ignition engine with a special head

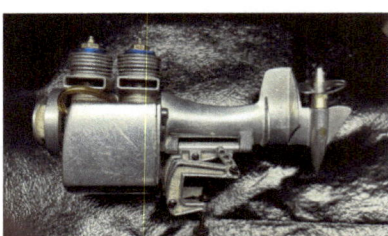

Sea Fury

that made it the most powerful engine on the market at that time. Later on I discovered eBay, and I participated in buying and selling engines and engine parts. This was a fascinating find as model airplane enthusiasts around the world participated in using this system. Once introduced to the engine collection hobby, I also found some unique motors for

Anderson Spitfire

model boats. My favorite turned out to be a twin cylinder, Sea Fury with an adjustable angle mount. This hobby has stayed with me forever. I have heard it mentioned many times that having a hobby in later years is beneficial in many ways. They say an active mind keeps the brain in better condition for remembering things.

Typically, by the middle of August, one had to think about heading back to the academic world. Moving back into our new rental place was always much easier than moving back into the fraternity house or helping the girls move into the dormitory. We did find out that by living at this house, we had a more time to focus on our studies, and still had time to have some fun.

I was a big football, basketball and wrestling fan, which was a good source of entertainment for me. The wrestling events were some of the best as that was when Dan Gable, Chris Taylor, Ben Petersen and several others made ISU well known in the wrestling world. The crowds were large and loud as the matches were always intense as everyone wanted to beat the best. The one item that I learned from watching the meets was that it pays to really keep focused if you want to do your best. Dan Gable was a prime example as he would not speak to anyone just prior to a match and his record was exceptional.

I decided to enter the teaching profession, during my 2nd year. I ended up doing student teaching at Perry, Iowa in biology for 6 weeks. I was assigned to work with a regular and an advanced group of students in biology. The approach and interaction with the students was quite different between the two groups, but both were quite interesting and rewarding in how they learned the subject matter. I will never forget one day at the school when I had a teacher from the junior high section came over and asked if I could take over his 7th grade class without any preparation. I agreed to do it, and it was probably the most fun day I had during the whole time on this project. This group of kids asked questions for the whole hour, and it was fun to turn it around and ask them questions that challenged their young, inquisitive minds as to how it effected their lives. For me, the best part of teaching was challenging these young minds to think and interact in active discussions as the world of biology is quite diverse and changing. Interesting enough, I was offered a teaching position at Story City, Iowa the same day I was offered a graduate study position with Dr. John Dunleavy in the Plant Pathology Department at Iowa State with a half-time job during the school year and full-time position in the summer. It was a very tough decision, but the graduate school won out as I enjoyed the challenge of finding solutions to new problems.

Ray and I finished our studies at ISU in the spring of 1965, and immediately after graduation I went with him back to Closter, NJ with him to go to the World's Fair. It was quite an experience for an old farm boy to be among millions of people and the subway was just like I pictured it – when the doors opened – it was a mass exit and entry! One of the exciting side activities was going to the famous Palisades Park. I was watching the roller coaster and I made the comment that one had to be crazy to ride that. Ten minutes later I was on it. The first downhill did just take my breath away! I survived and overall, it was a fantastic ride! Ray was a terrific host as he took me to the World Fair in New York and to the famous Radio City Music Hall. After the performance, we toured Times Square on foot and at that time it was like the city never slept. The following day we took a fairy around Stanton Island and then went to the Empire State Building. I stayed at Ray's house the whole week and I learned a lot about the plumbing business in New Jersey. His folks were very similar to mine They were very hard workers and very family orientated. Ray's mom was a good cook. She made a leg of lamb meal that really topped off a fantastic week.

Graduate School – Master's Program

Starting graduate school also meant that I needed to find a new apartment along with Herman as he was planning on going into veterinary medicine. We did find a basement apartment approximately a half-mile from campus. Within the first 6 months after moving in, Herman was diagnosed with prostate cancer and went back to Connecticut for treatment. Unfortunately, the cancer was very progressive and he passed away shortly after starting treatments. It was very hard for his parents as they ran a dog kennel, and I am sure they would have liked to have had Herman start up a veterinary office in that area. They did come to visit me in Ames and they also went to our farm. They were really nice people and they enjoyed visiting with my parents since they had a lot in common with them. My mother had to tell them about the times Herm was there at Easter, and she gave him the job of planting potatoes. At the end of that first year, I decided to find a new place to stay, and I was fortunate to find a nice two bedroom farmhouse to rent approximately 5 miles from work.

My major professor, Dr. John Dunleavy, worked half-time for the University and the other half for the USDA. The major crop that John was working on was soybeans. He was evaluating the incidence of Brown Stem Rot in the state of Iowa. It was a major issue at the time, and I remember they were testing the effect of rotation verses continuous planting of soybeans on the level of brown stem rot present. We had a long-term study for this project located at the Iowa State Agronomy Farm.

Soybean plants in 1966 were observed both in the greenhouse and in the field that displayed unusual symptoms that were characteristic of no previously described soybean disease. The disease was widespread and caused concern among Iowa soybean growers. My masters program was initiated to study this disease with the final title being "Stunting of Soybeans by *Pythium debaryanum and Pythiun ultium*".

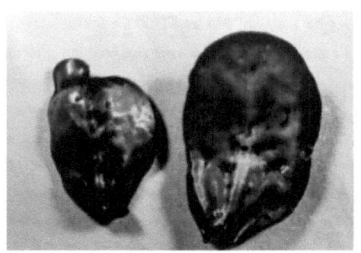  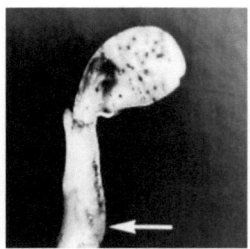

Lesions on the Cotyledons   Severe stunting   Swelling of the
                                                            Hypocotyl

The results of lab studies, screening of soybean varieties and extensive field studies indicated that Pythium debaryanum was the causal agent of the previously undescribed symptoms of a disease in Iowa. It produced dry lesions on the cotyledons, death of the apical meristem followed by development of axillary shoots and a swelling of the hypocotyl. Infected plants were severely stunted and the stand was markedly reduced. The stand was increased when treated with Panogen 15.

A greenhouse screening experiment revealed differences among 91 soybean varieties in their response to *Pythium debaryanum*. The range in vigor reduction from the resistant to the susceptible varieties was from 0 to 61%. These findings were quite important since almost every piece of ground that is used for crop production has a presence of these organisms. The population of Pythium in the soil can vary depending on the crop being grown. For example, continuous cropping of soybeans will tend to have higher populations and if the soybeans are planting in moist conditions where you can get compaction, the disease will be worse.

In addition to my research field plots, Dr. Dunleavy also had research projects for the USDA, and consequently, extra help was required in addition to his full-time manager, Jerry Fisher. It was at this time that they hired my brother Dan to help in the field planting of soybeans with hand planters, plot notes, harvesting and lab work. It was a great opportunity for Dan to experience, totally different environment than what he was used to at the farm. The research department where we worked had graduate students from all over the world and there was always interaction between groups, so Dan did get exposed to a lot of new ideas. Dan had lost total use of his right arm during our polio episode, however, that did not stop him from taking on this work project. One would almost get the impression that those of us with a physical activity have an extra incentive to prove that we can get the job done.

During our stay in Ames, we did establish lasting friendships and did some interesting activities like hunting for morel mushrooms in the Boone area. We became good friends with Jerry and Dodi Fisher who not only lived in this area, but Jerry also was the main technician for my major professor and would use Dan in the field activities. They were also animate about playing cards at night and we did that quite often It reminded us of playing cards with the neighbors back at the farm. In addition they would usually end up with a good supply of mushrooms that they were willing to share with us.

One of the other favorite things to do was to have poker games with some of the professors and other graduate students during the week. It was a very diverse group and the game selections were just as diverse. They ranged from 19-39 on or over to Jacks or better with three of a kind to win. Everyone took turns at hosting the games, although they did like to come out to the country where nobody got disturbed with the noise. I found it extremely interesting in that some of the professors that were extremely smart in their chosen field, did not use good judgement in some of the wild games that were chosen by the dealer. This was good for the struggling grad students and maybe they were just trying to help us out, but I don't think so. It was also very common for us to have card games during the noon lunch hour at Bessy Hall. This involved the supply room manager, students, and technicians. Outside of playing a lot of cards, we did go to class and did work in the lab. The classes in graduate school were generally much more constructive in that they were usually involved with your major and most, if not all the students, were there for the same reason. This is also where you got some of the top professors, and most of them were interested in helping with your research project if you needed some advice.

I found out that one of the benefits of majoring in plant pathology was that it involved all the major areas of biology including mycology, bacteriology, plant physiology, entomology, and virology. I minored in agronomy making a complete package that I would take advantage of later. During this time, I had the opportunity to meet some of the top professors in their field of study. It was a pleasure to listen to them talk about issues without a written lesson and just relying on actual hands-on experiences. It was a totally different atmosphere than during undergraduate study.

I did finish my graduate work on the effects of Pythium on soybeans, and did have a chance to present my findings to a group of plant pathologists at a meeting in Washington, D.C. I think this was the real start of interacting with scientists from around the world and how the disease pressures varied between different areas and different environmental conditions. I did enjoy doing the Master's program and did get asked to follow-up with a Doctorate's program.

Doctorate Program – Growing Bacteria-free Soybean Plants Under Gnotobiotic Conditions

My Master's work with Dr. Dunleavy left me with the clear perception that he did tend to let his imagination drive his thinking above the normal and out of the ordinary. For example, he previously isolated high populations of bacteria from actively growing soybean plants and did theorize that the mitochondria in soybean plants originated or acted like bacillus bacteria that were also rod-shaped in appearance like the mitochondria and were able to perform biochemical processes like those found in plants. The concept of research dealing with the development of bacteria-free plants or animals is primarily based on the premise that a microorganism can be physically separated from all microorganisms. The origin of this concept is not definite, but it probably began with the concepts of pure food and water and the realization that microbes might be involved in the health of man. Research involving development of bacteria-free plants or animals is an extension of the pure culture concept that an organism must be isolated from the natural complex state in which it normally exists if the demands of the experimental approach are to be satisfied.

To determine if the bacteria associated with the soybeans had a beneficial, neutral or detrimental effect on soybean growth, Dr. Dunleavy's suggestion for my graduate work was to devise a system where we could grow soybeans under gnotobiotic conditions, which meant that we would grow soybeans where we knew all the organisms involved inside the plant. That also meant that the soybeans would have to be grown in a sterile environment.

The first issue was to determine how does one start with a bacteria-free plant. Treating soybean seed with sodium hypocrite (NaOCl) eliminated all the bacteria in the cotyledons and seed coat, but it did not eliminate all the fungi. Excision of the embryo axis and discarding the cotyledons and seed coat eliminated all fungal contaminants. Any bacteria or fungi previously isolated from soybeans by Dr. Dunleavy, using similar media, were not isolated from the bacteria-free plants grown in this study. In addition, no bacterial protoplasts were isolated on horse serum agar which was used by Dr. Dunleavy to isolate bacterial protoplasts from soybeans. Consequently, the first step was to isolate the embryo from the cotyledon and since this was a food source, the embryo would have to be placed on an agar medium with nutrients added.

Once the embryo axis was excised in a Microvoid Transfer Hood, they were placed in agar container flasks to start the growth of the embryos. Once they started to grow, they were then transferred to the growth chamber through a special sleeve where everything was sterilized with a spray solution. The growth isolator had long sleeves with gloves on the end, and were good size – 61 cm x 97 cm x 97 cm. They were fastened to a plywood base which was placed on a cart with a flat top. An air blower was placed below on a second shelf. Light was supplied by 8 overhead cool-white, preheat, 40 W fluorescent bulbs. Air temperature in the units was kept at 25 degrees Centigrade.

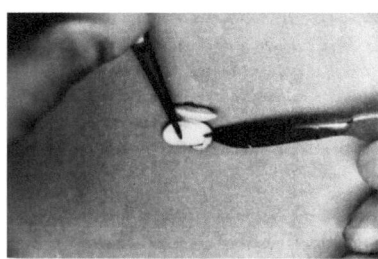

Excising the soybean embryo

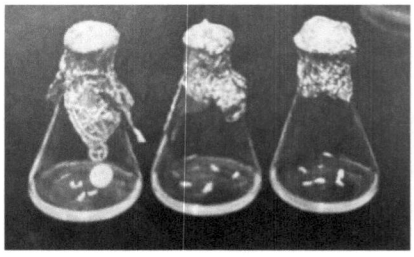

Erlenmeyer flasks with the excised embryo

Microvoid Transfer Hood

Microvoid Transfer Hood

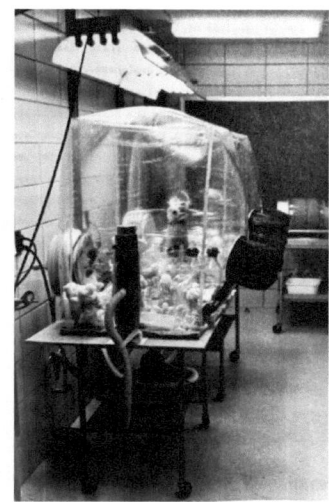

Growth Chamber

The isolators were sterilized by spraying the interior with 50-100 ml of peracetic acid solution (PAA). Non-autoclavable material was also placed in the isolator and sterized with the same solution. They were then left unused for 12 hours after spraying before the fan was turned on. The isolator was then vented for 5 days. Autoclavable material to be transferred into the isolators was places in a stainless-steel cylinder which was covered with mylar film and was autoclaved twice for 50 minutes at 121 degrees Centigrade. Following autoclaving, the cylinder was attached to the isolator by means of a vinyl transfer sleeve. The transfer sleeve was sprayed with PAA and was not used for 30 minutes. The double door locks were then removed and the mylar film was cut with a scalpel. A set of tongs was then used to reach into the cylinder to transfer the material inside the chamber.

Soybean seeds in isolator 1 were sterilized with NaOCl for 30 minutes before they were transferred to the isolator. Inside the isolator, a total of 50 Ford soybeans seeds were germinated in white sand in 8 cm and 10 cm clay pots. Howell's nutrient solution was added as needed. Plants from excised embryo axis were also used in isolator 1 (40 plants), and exclusively in isolator 2 (48 plants). These plants were excised from seed that was treated with the NaOCl for 30 minutes. The plants were grown in the dark in 250- and 500-ml Erlenmeyer flasks for 1 week before they were transferred to the isolators. Howell's nutrient solution was added to the flasks once a week after the agar began to dry.

The bacteria-free Ford and Blackhawk soybean plants were obtained by excising the embryo axis from seed that was treated with 2.63% NaOCl for 30 minutes. These embryos rapidly developed a white lateral root system in agar when either 0.3 ppm or 10 ppm gibberellic acid was added to the growth medium. The gibberellic acid, at a concentration of 10 ppm, also stimulated epicotyl elongation and expansion of the unifoliolate leaves.

Lateral root development was partially inhibited with 10 ppm streptomycin added to the growth medium and was completely inhibited with 50 ppm. In medium without streptomycin, 13 lateral roots/plant within 8 days after excision of the embryo axis. Only 5 lateral roots/plant occurred in medium with 10 ppm streptomycin.

Bacterial populations associated with excised embryos from normal seed not only inhibited lateral root formation, but also limited radicle elongation and generally produced a brown to black lesion on the radicle. The bacterial population also had a negative effect on the enzyme activity of young developing plants. The bacteria-free plants had a higher peroxidase and transaminase activity than normal plants which contained bacteria. Peroxidase activity has been closely associated with the metabolic processes which control the growth and development of plants.

The isolators were sterilized by spraying the interior with 50-100 ml of peracetic acid solution (PAA). Non-autoclavable material was also placed in the isolator and steiilized with the same solution. They were then left unused for 12 hours after spraying before the fan was turned on. The isolator was then vented for 5 days. Autoclavable material to be transferred into the isolators was places in a stainless-steel cylinder which was covered with mylar film and was autoclaved twice for 50 minutes at 121 degrees Centigrade. Following autoclaving, the cylinder was attached to the isolator by means of a vinyl transfer sleeve. The transfer sleeve was sprayed with PAA and was not used for 30 minutes. The double door locks were then removed and the mylar film was cut with a scalpel. A set of tongs was then used to reach into the cylinder to transfer the material inside the chamber.

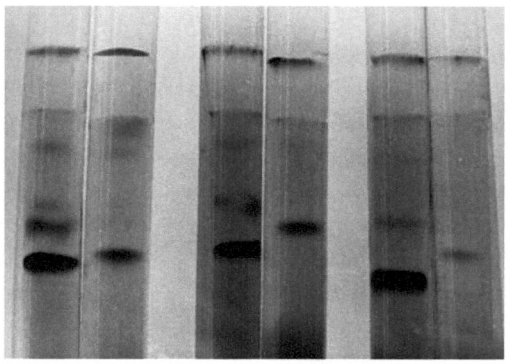

Peroxidase Activity in Three Soybean Varieties

Bacteria-free Corsoy   Normal Corsoy   Bacteria-free Harley   Normal Harley   Bacteria-free Ford   Normal Ford

Soybean seeds in isolator 1 were sterilized with NaOCl for 30 minutes before they were transferred to the isolator. Inside the isolator, a total of 50 Ford soybeans seeds were germinated in white sand in 8 cm and 10 cm clay pots. Howell's nutrient solution was added as needed. Plants from excised embryo axis were also used in isolator 1 (40 plants), and exclusively in isolator 2 (48 plants). These plants were excised from seed that was treated with the NaOCl for 30 minutes. The plants were grown in the dark in 250- and 500-ml Erlenmeyer flasks for 1 week before they were transferred too the isolators. Howell's nutrient solution was added to the flasks once a week after the agar began to dry.

The bacteria-free Ford and Blackhawk soybean plants were obtained by excising the embryo axis from seed that was treated with 2.63%

NaOCl for 30 minutes. These embryos rapidly developed a white lateral root system in agar when either 0.3 ppm or 10 ppm gibberellic acid was added to the growth medium. The gibberellic acid, at a concentration of 10 ppm, also stimulated epicotyl elongation and expansion of the unifoliolate leaves.

Lateral root development was partially inhibited with 10 ppm streptomycin added to the growth medium and was completely inhibited with 50 ppm. In medium without streptomycin, 13 lateral roots/plant within 8 days after excision of the embryo axis. Only 5 lateral roots/plant occurred in medium with 10 ppm streptomycin.

Bacterial populations associated with excised embryos from normal seed not only inhibited lateral root formation, but also limited radicle elongation And generally produced a brown to black lesion on the radicle. The bacterial population also had a negative effect on the enzyme activity of young developing plants. The bacteria-free plants had a higher peroxidase and transaminase activity than normal plants which contained bacteria.

In summary, the bacteria-free plants developed normally under gnotobiotic conditions. No fungi, bacteria, or bacteria protoplasts were detected in an isolator used exclusively to grow plants from the excised embryo axis. I know this was a lot of detail that most readers would not be interested in, but it does provide one with the concept of how complicated the plant world can be and a glimpse of how a project like this one provides a multitude of different learning parameters for a graduate student. I thoroughly enjoyed it and the concept of identifying the interaction of organisms and keeping an open mind as to what might be feasible in the biological world is something that has followed me through a lifetime.

Postdoc Position

Following the completion of my Ph.D. program, I was asked to do a two-year program working full time on a soybean project for my major professor. I readily accepted the position as my professor was always thinking out-of-the-box, and that always got my attention. The work environment for this project was just excellent as there were all kinds of activity at this location.

Close to our lab in Bessy Hall was another research lab working on corn. I met one of the graduate students and his name was Mike Turner who was married to Beth Ann Lung from Denver, Colorado. We established a close relationship after that first meeting. Mike had no interest in participating in our poker games, but he did enjoy movies, dinners, and in one case, he played in our plant pathology football game in October. That was a lot of fun as Mike was very tall, and as a short quarterback, I could throw any kind of pass his way as there were no tall defenders. That was a fun game for me as this guy cannot run! After the football game, Beth decided that I should meet her younger sister, Dorothy, who lived in Denver. Two months later during Christmas time, the Turners invited her to visit them for the holidays. It was at that time that we had our first date, and it was to the movie "Love Story". After several dinners and visits that week, Dorothy returned to Denver to go back to work. She was employed by the Smith Tool Company that made drill bits for oil wells in Texas. Dorothy lived with her mother, Pauline, and she had a younger sister there named Deborah.

After the Christmas meeting in Ames, Dorothy and I communicated by mail. The following August I rode a BSA 441 motorcycle out to

Sturgis, SD for the big motorcycle rally. After the Rally, I then rode to Denver to see Dorothy. Her mother was on the shy side. She was a hard worker, and probably wondering how her daughter ever ended up with this crazy guy. However, it did not take her long to know that I was just a good ole farm boy from Iowa. She did warn Dorothy that she would have to really cook a lot of steak for this guy as she thought I had expensive tastes since I took them to the Jefferson 440 club for dinner.

In addition to taking them to dinner, I did take Dorothy on a long motorcycle ride through the Rocky Mountains. The bike had a long narrow seat that was not comfortable for the rider, but she was a real sport and did not complain at all.

I went back to my work at Iowa State, and three months later, I did propose to Dorothy in Ames. She accepted, but she did request that we wait until she had her Ford Falcon paid off first. I agreed and we set the date for July 8, 1972, in Lakewood, Colorado.

In Dorothy's younger years, she worked for a Jewish family, Ed and Rae Ann Lampert, that she really enjoyed. And after meeting them, they became part of our family as well. They had two boys, Mark and Lee and one daughter, Vicki, that Dorothy would take care of in their younger years. One of their favorite pastimes was to chase firetrucks to a fire. This family is a fun group to say the least, and it was yet another culture that I had never been exposed to before. I found it to be fun and exciting. This is another example of friends forever!

Dorothy's dad started his career in radio at the U.S. Air Force Base in Utah in 1942. After a short tour of duty there, he was transferred to Lowry Air Force Base in Denver, Colorado, where he supervised all radio communications with over one hundred civilian and military personnel under his command. At the end of 1946, he opened his own radio and television business and was quite successful repairing electronic equipment. Unfortunately, he passed away with lung cancer before I got a chance to meet him. Consequently, Dorothy did ask Ed Lampert to give her away at our wedding.

The wedding announcement was quite exciting for my folks, although there was cause for anxiety as my mother was not use to traveling and having to spend nights in a motel room. It did turn out to be a great trip for them and they even did some touring during their stay in Denver. My best man was my roommate from college, Ray Dorow. Also part of the wedding party was Charles Boeck who has been a lifelong friend from Denison. The wedding was well planned by all the sisters and it was to take place in Dorothy's church. I did have to add a little excitement to the event prior to the wedding. Dorothy's boss decided to treat us to a luncheon, and we celebrated it with a special drink called a Fog Cutter. It turned out that I had an allergic reaction to the drink and my lip swelled up tremendously. Fortunately, a cortisone shot by a doctor got everything back to normal before the ceremony. The wedding went as planned and a great reception followed the wedding to make the event very memorable.

Adam, Deborah. Pauline, Beth, Dorothy   Dorothy   Dorothy   Ed Lampert

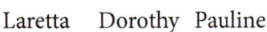

Laretta   Dorothy Pauline   Pauline   Dorothy

73

Beth   Dorothy Deborah   Wedding Cake

Deborah   Mallory   Ray Dorow   Dorothy   Doc   Beth   Charles Boeck

We started our married life by staying in downtown Denver the first night, and then the next morning we left on an organized tour to Hawaii. I always had reservations about going with a tour package, but I got brave and signed us up for it. Our first stop was in San Francisco where we would change planes. Since we had a long layover, we decided to get ready for Hawaii by having a Mia Tai before we boarded the next flight. On this next flight which was about four hours in length, part of the package deal was that we did get a free drink along with a steak dinner. Naturally, we ordered a Mia Tai prior to the dinner.

Apparently, it was a strong drink as Dorothy decided that when the dinner arrived, she did not feel up to par so I had to eat her steak also. Another one of those events that got talked about a lot in later years. Once we arrived in Honolulu and got off the plane to receive an orchid necklace, everything was fine and Dorothy was ready to have fun. The smell of the orchid was fantastic and something one would remember.

We stayed at the Hilton Hawaiian Hotel and the next morning we had a group meeting where you could decide what activities you would like to participate in during the week. The advantage to this program was that several events were sold out unless you signed up at this meeting. The Don Ho Dinner Show was one of those. We did sign up for that one as I was always a fan of Don Ho and the show turned out to be a good one. We also signed up to fly to the big island of Hawaii, the Fern Grotto tour, a tour of the city and a beach party. One of the things I always remembered from the trip was the laid-back attitude of the tour guides. When we went on a boat trip up to the Fern Grotto, it was one singing affair and a lot of fun. When we visited the big island, we did collect some of the lava rock from the volcano and we still have it in our back yard. Overall, the tour package was well organized and we had a lot of fun. Now, it was time to get back to Denison and start working.

View from the Hilton Hawaiian Hotel

Dorothy and Doc in Hawaii

Start of a New Era

Our first place of residence was a large apartment on the second floor above a financial business in the center part of Denison. At that time, I did not have a job in my profession so I took on part time jobs like helping Paul Losh restore the Dodge House in Dow City, helping at the farm, and driving a farm couple who had needed assistance with obtaining supplies. Dorothy took on a part-time job at a local grocery store, so we basically made it work. I did not think about it at the time, but this lifestyle was different from the environment that she grew up while in Denver. One of the key differences noted was that in a small rural community, everybody knew everybody and what they did for a living. That was totally different for her and one of those items that was hard to get use to at the time. I know we did go to Omaha occasionally just so she could get a taste of the hustle and bustle of the city. I think for some of us and maybe most people the art of communicating is a constant learning endeavor at least for one person I know by the name of Doc. Fortunately in our case, we both were determined to make the most of it.

In about 6 months, I did get a job with a new company that decided to start their business in Denison. Most of the people involved were from the east coast of all places. The name of the company was Environment 2000 LTD and their original objective was to design and sell a biological control agent to save the pet turtle industry that was in danger due to Salmonella transmission to humans. I was hired to head up the research effort to find a solution. One of the potential control agents was to find a bacteriophage that would kill the Salmonella. I sampled the pits of several swine confined feeding operations and I did isolate some bacteriophage that would kill the Salmonella species that currently was the problem. The lab facilities were very good and basically this process required a lot of testing that required a lot of time. I remember the stock for this company started at $2 per share and within a short period of time it was at $23 per share. There was a lot of interest in biological control and a lot of potential. The challenge that eventually ended the project was that the Salmonella bacteria mutated very easily. It was impossible to develop a biological control agent that would eliminate all strains. The company closed shortly after two years.

During our work with the original project, I also had started working on a water clarifier for aquariums and farm ponds. It was simply using aluminum sulfate to precipitate out the phosphorus which eliminated the algae from growing. It was very effective, and one company did pick up on how good it was. It was called "Brite N Clear" for use in aquariums.

After I had started working at Environment 2000, we moved to a small house on 5th Avenue North. It was owned by my parents and it was the right size to get started with at this time. We also decided that maybe it was time to start a family now that I had secured a full-time job. On July 4th, 1974, we had our first daughter, Shannon. She was 7 lbs. 4 ounces. There was a lot of excitement over this event, especially since my mother was convinced that we could not have girls as she had lost both of her little girls at an early age. One was my twin, Judy, Who had an open spine and only lived for a few weeks At this time my folks were very helpful and had some good pointers for us new parents. It was amazing how many challenges arrived with parenting, so we were grateful for all the assistance.

The next two years were quite busy as we started the parenting process as well as keeping busy at Environment 2000. In addition, Dorothy's sisters along with many other friends did stop by for a visit. During the summer, we did some motorcycle riding, raised and sold sweet corn and spent time boating at Lake View with my brother Dan and the folks. During the summer, a lot of Sundays were spent at the lake cooking out and having a good time boating.

Dorothy did take Shannon out to Denver when she was only two to show her to her mom. Shortly after arriving, Dorothy called and said

Shannon was quite sick and they were going to admit her in the hospital. Dan and I drove out to Denver to help, and upon arrival, I went to Children's Hospital and the first thing I encountered was Shannon in a room with a bunch of young nurses trying to get an IV put in her head. There was blood everywhere, and it was just a mess! Somehow, she survived and eventually everything turned out okay, but it was one of those events that a person never forgets.

When we got back to Denison, Shannon was thrilled to see the "Duck" on top of a local restaurant. For some reason, she found this bird on the top of the restaurant fascinating and every time we drove by, she would get excited. It was a chicken, but a duck to her!

When August came around, we got ready to travel to the Sturgis Rally in South Dakota. Dorothy and I had the 650 BSA loaded down with a lot of luggage and were headed to Hot Springs when suddenly the rear tire blew out. It was a two-lane highway and there was a car coming from the opposite direction. I laid the cycle down on the right side and just stayed on top of it. Dorothy did not stay on and thank goodness she had a helmet on. It was obvious her arm was broken, along with a pavement road rash. Fortunately, we were able to get an ambulance to take us to the hospital at Rapid City, South Dakota.

I lost a lot of skin on both arms, but nothing was broken. Evidently, there had been a crash earlier on that highway, and they had not cleaned up all the glass. Unknowingly, I drove through the glass and the synthetic inner tube that I had put in the rear tire did not react like a rubber tube. Instead of a slow release of air, it rips and acts as a blowout! Another hard lesson learned. We did spend a couple of days at the Rapid City hospital and then went to Sturgis to wait for someone to bring our car out to take us home. Unfortunately, instead of recovering, new challenges showed up.

Dorothy's broken arm was not healing and they discovered bone fragments in her sinus cavities. It was decided that she should go to Methodist Hospital in Omaha to have surgery. After the lab/prep work, they told us she was pregnant. We were not ready for that and then we had to decide if we should proceed with the surgery. We decided the surgery was necessary and everything did turn out okay. Now, there was the issue of an arm that was not healing. One option was to have surgery to scrape the bone and re-adjust it. We did not like to take the risk of another surgery, so we decided to try something entirely different.

A doctor in Omaha introduced us to a new device that would fit around your upper arm, and when you plugged It in, it would create a magnetic field that was supposed to stimulate bone growth. You were supposed to leave it plugged in for 10 hours per day. That presented a real challenge as she had a two-year old daughter that wanted her attention also, but she did it for 6 months.

We went in for checkups every month and for the first several months we did not see anything too positive. Dorothy had more patience and perseverance than I ever thought of having. Then, after 6 months, the doctor came in and said it was healed. The doctor was surprised that it worked!

We never did talk or hear of anybody else who used this technique, but it did work for us. Now it was time to get ready for daughter number 2!

On May 14, 1976, Vicki Lynn arrived in full glory. I was in the delivery room having a good conversation with the doctor, and suddenly, he was catching Miss Vicki! The doctor then proceeded to tell me that I will need to talk to Dorothy as Vicki had characteristics not like dad! She had a dark complexion and dark hair. After 45 years, I would have to say the doctor was wrong as she is a clone of her dad. It is almost scary!

In approximately 15 months, another super bundle arrived on July 25, 1977! This was Jeri Renae ready to set the world on fire! This changed Grandma's thoughts on the possibility of us having girls. We were so blessed to end up with three fantastic daughters! They had their own characteristics that evolved into many, many stories. I will try to capture the ones that stood out to us at the time. Grandma and Grandpa Strissel could not get enough of spending time with them! Grandpa would take the girls to have coffee with the boys and Grandma would play cards with them at 2:00 in the morning. Christmas was always a special time with treats and presents. Other key activities included going boating, fishing, motorcycle riding, playing at the farm, dancing, going to hill climbs and even trips to the Sturgis Motorcycle Rally.

The closing of Environment 2000 LTD was quite disappointing to many including me, however, another individual from Storm Lake, Iowa purchased the building and hired me to run the lab working on another biological extract. The next business that followed in the same building was the Dawn Corporation. This company was involved with making an extract from ocean kelp that contained growth hormones. The original intent was to use it in the flower industry however, I expanded it to include field crops such as corn and soybeans along with vegetables. In addition to the kelp project, we did rat bait for B&N Products in Harlan, Iowa.

The project with kelp was very interesting. I tested it on corn, soybeans, tomatoes, cucumbers, melons and cabbage. There wasn't any doubt that it stimulated a plant response, but it was different for different crops. For melons and cabbage, it would increase the size. For tomatoes and cucumbers, it would enhance the maturity process so that more were ripe at the same time. The extract would increase yield in soybeans, but on corn, if it was a good year and everything was in balance, then it was difficult to show a yield increase. If it was under stress, then there was an advantage. It was a great product, but market wise it was tough to promote when economic times were tough and any extra money farmers would have did not go to these type of products.. The owner closed the business and moved to Kansas City. During this time, I had made contacts with people in the animal health market which would lead me to my next job in Fremont, Nebraska.

Ag America

In 1979, we moved to Fremont, NE where I went to work for a pharmaceutical company called Ag America. The owner was Bob Wendt who was doing a lot of contract work for Allied Mills in Chicago. Dorothy and I purchased a house in a new housing area on the west side of Fremont. We did all the finish work on the inside of the house including the kitchen cabinets. It turned out to be a great ranch house with a full basement and a fireplace.

Our neighbors soon became great friends, and we lived in a neighborhood were everyone was about the same age and they enjoyed getting together to have fun. There would be days where one neighbor would stop by to see what you were working on, then another one would stop by, and then other neighbors came, and we soon would have a party. It was just a lot of fun. The neighbors had girls the same age as ours, so that made it fun for them also. Grandma, Grandpa, and Dan would also join us on several weekends.

Ag America had a manufacturing plant in downtown Fremont. They manufactured a lot of animal health products for other companies such as Allied Mills in Chicago. At that time, I was basically in charge of quality control as it was a critical part in this business. This was not what my professional training was for, but it was a good job and I did get to meet some professional people who provided me with some excellent advice on contracting the production of a product for another company. The key person I met concerning contracting was Bill Wittern from

Allied Mills in Chicago. This was a key factor for me as I learned that there are a lot of professionals that you can create a great networking I learned relationship that could have many benefits. that if you surround yourself with good people, you will be successful.

One of our neighbors became good friends in that we did a lot of activities with them for many years. Dave and Coke Wolthuis had very similar interests to ours and they had two girls that were similar in age to our girls. Dorothy enjoyed working with people and having friends that you could trust and share information with. Dave and I had a similar relationship and had great times playing golf, poker, and just talking about business.

Another great family next door was Steve and Jan Shudak who also had girls similar in age to ours. Steve was a good poker player that always would join in our games as well as other neighborhood gatherings. All these people would help with anything happening and have a good time doing it. I have not

Dave

Coke   Kelly   Rona

experienced another neighborhood like that one. It appears that there is more separation of people now than ever. I am sure there are still isolated examples of what we found in Fremont, but in general, the overall trend is headed in a different direction.

In august of 1981, I was contacted by Dennis Stamp offering employment with Wilson Seeds in Harlan, Iowa. The work consisted of selecting corn and soybean products for their sales department. It also involved traveling to evaluate plant disease and agronomic problems in their commercial fields. This was an opportunity to work again in my profession, and I accepted the position.

The company had a trailer house that I could use until we found some living quarters in Harlan. Dorothy stayed back in Fremont to sell the house that ended up selling by the following January. At that time, Dorothy moved into the trailer with me until we could find a house to buy or rent. Our new move did not start the best as I was on a sales trip to northern Iowa and got stranded due to a snowstorm. In the meantime, the storm hit Harlan also, and the strong wind kept blowing out the gas furnace in the trailer. This was a new issue for Dorothy, and she basically had to find someone to come in to take care of the problem. The person she found was an old timer that basically rolled up some newspaper and started it on fire to ignite the furnace. It scared her something awful. We felt fortunate to have the trailer, but it was small for our family, and it only had one exit door. If there would have been a fire in the front, we would not have been able to get out. Consequently, we were anxious to find a house.

Fortunately, it was not long after that, we did find a house to buy in Harlan. It was a three-bedroom ranch house with the Pioneer Park adjacent to our back yard. The perk offered a nice area for the girls to play and practice tumbling. It had a playground and a one mile walking trail. There was also a pond that attracted large flocks of Canadian geese.

One of the first things we did in the house was to make a restroom downstairs with three mirrors. This was a great investment as later when the girls were in dance, or had friends over for prom, or birthdays there was always a gathering in that room. In time, we remodeled the whole basement into two offices, a TV area, a storage area, and a laundry room.

I could write a whole book on the family life I experienced in for more than 50 years, but I am going to limit it to just a few of the stories, observations and opinion of raising three daughters. There is one story that warrants some time here. One time, Dorothy and I went uptown to watch my dad play in a pool tournament, and grandma Strissel was watching all three girls at our house. Grandma had all three girls on the floor of the living room teaching them to play poker with chips. Unannounced, the pastor from our church came to visit that night. Needless to say, grandma was embarrassed. The best part, however, was the following Sunday when she went to church with us. After the service it is a common practice for the pastor to greet everyone. When he saw grandma Strissel, he greeted her as that poker playing grandma. If anyone had a red face, it was grandma!

Everyone has a different opinion on the value or experience of having a family. For me, it made life have some real meaning and I had loads of fun doing it. There were always challenges to overcome, but with a good partner, they were overcome. For us, we did establish an unending close relationship with our daughters throughout their school years and now into their new adventures. I do not want to project that we never had arguments or misunderstandings, because we did. The key was that everyone would always look for a solution and that is what made it work for us. I had one high school counselor ask me what was the key to our success in raising these three girls. I don't pretend to have the magic answer, but I am going to tell you a few of my key observations. I do know that creating a family unit like the one we had was the highlight of my career. In addition, we also expanded a positive relationship with all the girl cousins. The level of only our closeness increased when the grandkids started to arrive, and now, I have even reached the status of being a great grandfather. All I can say is that the experience has been fantastic. To this book, I am just going to cover a few aspects of raising my daughters.

Jeri Vicki Dorothy Doc Shannon

Jeri   Shannon   Vicki

Shannon   Jeri   Vicki

Doc's current extended family

Observations of Raising a Family of Girls

In looking back over time, I think my first key observation was that all my girls attended Sherri and Juli's dance and gymnastic classes at an early age. Dorothy was very instrumental in getting this process started. Fortunately, both instructors were top notch in not only knowing the program, but were good at keeping the kids in line, motivated and tuned

Vicki   Jeri   Shannon

in to what was needed to put on a good performance. They received additional experience by traveling to other cities for competition events. One of the side benefits was that they got to meet and interact with many other kids. The dance groups would also go to care centers on special holidays to put on a show for the older generation. I don't know how much credit to give this endeavor but our daughters were always able to talk to adults with ease, In addition, they did spend a lot of time playing cards, going fishing, going boating and a special time was taking the girls to national motorcycle races like the Springfield Mile or the Sturgis Motorcycle rally. It was customary for us that after the national race event was over to take the girls down to meet the racers and in many cases get their autograph. Not to be forgotten, there were the annual Easter egg hunts at the farm.

Vicki, Rocky and Grandpa Strissel   Ricky Graham signing Jeri's shirt

Ricky Graham   Vicki   Easter Egg Hunt at the farm

Vicki   Chris Carr   Vicki

Vicki   Shannon   Jeri

My second key observation was that the girls got involved with 4-H and a lot of school activities that allowed them to get more involved with other kids. In my opinion, this made them much more adaptable to working out solutions dealing with kids with different ideas or cultures. In the school system the girls became very involved in many activities. Vicki was a major participant with the track and cross country program. In addition to also being a cheer leader, she was a member of the homecoming court. Jeri was involved with the POM POM Squad, the Flag Corps and tennis. She also won the Optimist Appreciation Award. Shannon was very active with the band and a multi-denominational band group that would perform at various churches on Sundays during the school year. In addition, all the girls worked at a popular family type restaurant that attracted the older generation. The result was that the girls turned out to be very good workers, could interact very well with adults, were in good physical condition, and they knew what it took to make a living to support a family. In my opinion, there is one other key element and that is parental support. I know this concept becomes harder and harder to do in today's busy world, but I know it had a positive response for us.

Jeri

Shannon

Vicki

Shortly after we finished the house, Dorothy decided she would like a lap size dog to watch TV with. We were at a shopping mall in Sioux City we walked by a window in a pet store and this one cute puppy had his eyes on charming everyone, and he did. Therein starts the story of Quincy and being a Lhasa Apso, he should not get too big. Well, Quincy turned out to be twice the size he should be even though he had papers and everything saying he was the real deal. Quincy had some unique characteristics that took us a long time to understand. One of his attention tricks was to lay close to a dog biscuit and wait for Shannon to walk by, and then he would attack her. The other girls could walk by and he would not do anything. In Asia, they are considered a guard dog, and he was a family dog. All visitors had to be introduced and then everything was fine.

When we would take him for a car ride, he would sit up front on Dorothy's lap and every time we would meet a car, Quincy would duck! He loved to eat sweet corn on the cob just like a human. He enjoyed hamburgers from Burger King and ice cream. He also had to have his dog food in a gravy form. During the school year, sometimes we had daughters that wanted to sleep In. I would take Quincy into the room to chew on some toes. That worked extremely well!!

One action that Quincy pulled was probably the highlight of our relationship. I came home one night from a Wilson's sales meeting and guess who was sleeping on my pillow? When I tried to move him all I would get is an angry growl. I was in the motion of putting his lights out, but Dorothy saved him, and I slept in the other room. That story was told many times in the following years.

20 Years with Wilson Genetics

I could probably write an entire book on all my experiences with Wilson Genetics, but I focused on some key events and lessons learned. I would have to say up front that working with a family-owned business was good in that today we are associated with another family-owned business in Argentina. They do have a different structure and attitude verses the large corporations. I found that members of the larger corporations were more intent on moving up the ladder than satisfying the customer needs. They did have more benefits in terms of money, retirement plans, and access to qualified help.

When I started working with Wilson Genetics, Dennis Stamp was the president, and they had sales reps in IA, NE, and KS. His wife, Jan, was a real asset as she helped with all the company functions, and she interacted very well with all the families of the sales reps. One of the things I learned from Dennis was that if you are going to do something, do it right. If you are going to make a technical sheet handout, make it look professional Dennis was always up front with me and told me exactly what he thought. I remember one time I told him that I knew his dad did not approve of my position with the company, and he said that is correct. There was no guessing about what was said.

The company also had a sales manager by the name of Steve Pierce who had a terrific personality and was fun to work with in supporting sales functions or training sessions. One year, Steve played Santa Claus, and I was an elf at the company's annual Christmas party. Well, we started the party by me pulling Santa Claus on to the stage in a red wagon, and wouldn't you know it, I upset the wagon and dumped Santa on the stage. You can guess that got the party started in grand style and everyone had a party to talk about for years.

The company was aggressive which I enjoyed a lot. In a short period of time, I was able to hire a plant breeder by the name of Dr. Pat Donahue. Pat was one of those individuals who was not only smart but could interact with anyone. Previously, we were using inbred material from a lot of foundation seed companies for product development, and then with Pat involved, we started our own nursery and created a series of new corn hybrids. Shortly after that we were purchased by a French cement company called Orsan. Their main interest was to find a solution to the fusarium stalk rot issue they had in France. At the time, they had made a contract with Dr. Elmer Johnson to help also. Elmer had worked for CIMMYPT in Mexico for 25 years and collected corn from all over the world. He then moved to San Francisco to work with the Internation Plant Research Institute using the material he had collected.

At that point, we started working intently with Elmer and then with breeders from France and Spain. We had a joint winter nursery in Argentina, where we would spend a week evaluating material for France, but also for our area. We also visited the nurseries in France and Spain to evaluate material for Europe. In the early stages, Elmer had started replicated yield trials in Minnesota that we would harvest for yield. After two years, the material all moved to the Midwest for testing. Elmer was a master at creating populations of corn, and he did provide me with a lot of material to work with in the future.

The change in ownership also brought in a new president by the name of John Crabtree. John could work with the group from France probably better than most. Orsan had a policy to bring in new people so that they could learn the seed business which was fine except that it did require a lot of extra time, and then they would move to a different location and another person would come in to be trained. They were very smart, but it was hard for them to understand how everything worked. For example, the first season they were here, our seed production field in Walnut, IA had zero yield due to the drought. They would constantly ask how can that be?

I continued to travel to all the sales districts to put on sales meetings during the winter and field days during the summer promoting both corn and soybean products. The side benefit to this was that I got to participate in fishing trips for the sales group and Dorothy and I got to travel to Mexico and Hawaii. That was a treat for us as we probably would not have gone there on our own. Our sales group did know how to have a good time so that made it a lot of fun. One year when we were in Hawaii, we did take the sales group to see our winter nursery. We took a boat over to the island where we had the nursery and, on the way over, we had the whales putting on a show for us all the way. The trips and entertainment events were always well planned. Pictured below are some pictures of our trip to Hawaii.

I also got to make a lot of sales trips to work with the sales division of Tech Ag de Mexico that was headed up by Manuel Sanchez. Manuel's agronomist, Genaro Muzquiz, who oversaw setting up several strip plots of our corn to evaluate in several areas in Mexico. This was very helpful as in some area they had a severe fusarium problem, and you could evaluate the material for tolerance or susceptibility. There were times when I had sorghum breeders from Texas tour the plots with us, and in one case, there was a breeder from South Africa that toured with us. One time, one of the dealers toured the plots with us and at the end of the day, his family hosted a party for us, and it so happened part of his business was in making tequila which he served at the party. It was quite good, and everyone had a good time. It was much better than one time I was traveling with Manuel and his sales group, and he stopped at a nice restaurant for lunch. Well, Manuel ordered a bowl of fish soup and when it was delivered, I had the head of a sick fish starring at me. This fish looked like a fish that had been laying on shore for three days and had that gray appearance.

Manuel Sanchez and Doc

Doc in Mexico

Snowmobiling in the Rocky Mountains

Doc in the Rocky Mountains

In summary, I certainly appreciate the fact that I had the opportunity to meet all the people that I did and get a chance to observe what growers need in the Midwest and other parts of the world. I also got the opportunity to travel and do things that I did not think I would ever do. I think one of the most fascinating things that I did was to learn how to ride a snowmobile in the Rocky Mountains. For most, it probably would be no big deal, but in my situation where I was limited in my walking ability, doing something in deep snow was an issue. During my travels in Nebraska for Wilson Genetics, I did some work with Jack Wendell who had 30 pivots under irrigation south of North Platte. Jack and his family were top notch and very progressive in their agriculture endeavors. One winter he invited me to his cabin in Meeker, Colorado to go snowmobiling. I took him up on the offer and had a great time. It did take me a little to determine the throttle was my best friend, but after that, it was all go and we ended up traveling 50 miles in the mountains.

Shortly after we were acquired by Orsan, we were traveling to Spain and France to tour the nurseries that their breeders were working at that time. In France, they were working on early hybrids and in Spain, they were working on hybrids with maturities like ours. After that initial visit, we all sat down and planned a joint winter nursery for planting in Argentina. This was an exciting time as we were now making crosses with very diverse genetics that favor the production of unique hybrids. In March of every year, we would meet in Argentina to evaluate the material and spend a week planning our next step. I really enjoyed traveling to Argentina as in some respects it was like going back 40 years in time. There was an ice cream store in the town where we stayed, and the owner drove a model A Ford to work every day. There was nine of us looking at the nursery and when we went to lunch, the total bill was $27.00 and that included dessert. At the end of the week, our hosts, Juan-Carlos Maggio and Miquel Guichandute would put on a luncheon that included grilling all different types of sausage. One of those happened to be a blood sausage that I had always heard my folks talk about in the old days, but no one ever fixed any of those anymore. There was another fascinating thing that I discovered while I was there. They don't eat dinner until 9:00 at night and they are ready to go to work at 7:00 a.m. They said that it kept the family more intact, and that there was much less crime overall. Another unusual event I had the opportunity of observing was a march of the Communist Party with machine guns through the shopping area of Buenos Aries. Later that night, a couple of blocks away, I went to a night club where I got to see a lot of dancers doing the tango. That was quite entertaining to see.

Before I leave this segment of my working career, there are a few encounters that I had that were so different for me that I never forgot them. One was a trip to Madrid Spain with Dr. Elmer Johnson and a young corn breeder I had just hired. We had toured downtown Madrid with a taxi driver, and he told us that before we went to the airport, we should eat at this one bar, so we did. The lunch special was fresh baby eels, so the young breeder and I ordered the special. They were cooked in olive oil and were about 3" long with a spaghetti appearance. The next morning the young breeder was telling me that he could not get to sleep as he kept seeing those eel eyes looking at him. On another occasion, I was with this same young breeder at a restaurant in Mexico City. For appetizers, we had corn smut and fried ant eggs. I had always heard that a lot of people in Mexico would eat corn smut, so I had to try it. It had no flavor, and I would not suggest having it. The ant eggs were quite good.

Another unique experience I had in my research endeavors, and another important lesson in life learned happened when I was working with a Wilson district manager in eastern Iowa. He asked me f I could supply white corn to a mission group near the equator, and I thought it was a good opportunity to evaluate some hybrids in a different environment. The young gentleman that planted the field would send me pictures as the crop grew and everything looked good. After harvest, I asked the sales manager how the corn finished. Well, he said the kernels were all shriveled at harvest. It turns out that when it got close to maturity, the rainy season started, and they did not want all the water to run down inside the ears so they went through the field and bent all the ears down. This of course shut off the flow of nutrients and water to the ear! I always try to anticipate what could happen, but there are always surprises along the way.

One of the fascinating things that came out of the work with Dr. Elmer Johnson's material was the development of a high protein yellow corn. It was one of those items that was very unique at the time, and it did get patented. In addition, we got major exposure by having it written up in a major seed industry magazine called Seed World. It was also introduced to the seed industry at the ASTA Meeting in Chicago that is attended by 2500 seedsmen from around the world. Another fascinating aspect to this was that a high protein white inbred was isolated from the same population of corn with similar characteristics. The white high protein inbred has opened a lot of new marketing opportunities.

Dr. G. Pollack   Doc   Dr. B. Kindiger

Start of JFS and Associates, LTD.

Approximately 8 years after Orsan purchased Wilson Genetics the company changed ownership again as Land O Lakes became a 50% owner. Then, in 2002, the company was purchased by Syngenta. I worked for three years in their research division on white corn. It was my first working experience within a large corporate structure. They certainly had some unique benefits, but I did make some of the same observations as I did with Orsan. I learned a lot working with them, and we had success working with the high protein white corn in a wet mill, and in trout feeding trials. Then, one day, we had a corporate meeting at their main headquarters in Minneapolis to determine what they were going to do with me as I was focused on non-GMO material and their mission was to focus on using traits. The result was that I left Syngenta and started JFS and Associates, LTD as I had several end-users that wanted me to develop propriety corn hybrids for them.

Braydi and Vicki   Braydi and Dorothy

There have been a lot of stories of how companies started in their garage, and this is another one. Dorothy and I started the business in our garage, and then shared a space in a commercial building for three years. Then we purchased a large warehouse type building in Harlan in 2009 and have continued to expand ever since. Help in the beginning consisted of Lyle Fiscus, my wife, Dorothy, and Randy Gessert. Eventually, my daughter, Vicki, and her daughters along with Darold Gessert, Marcia Gessert, Jo Petersen, and several other part-time helpers played a part in the growth of the company. Today, Vicki is now the CFO of the company, and a new addition is Ross Petersen who is the Genetic Support Specialist.

Peter   Juan   Sam   Lynn   Doc

The company is basically a seed foundation company which means it develops new inbred lines of corn for the seed industry to use in development of new corn hybrids. We have spent most of our time on white corn, but we decided to develop both white and yellow lines of corn. Early in our development we were introduced to another family run business from Argentina called Rusticana. They were a seed foundation company specializing in yellow flint corn and they were wanting to expand their business. We met with Peter Hyland and his dad, Sam in Des Moines, Iowa. From that time on, we have worked with their breeders on developing new corn hybrids. The person responsible for introducing us was Lynn Clarkson with Clarkson Grain in Cerro Gordo, IL. Lynn also happens to be the individual that introduced us to the tortilla industry in Chicago. The company he introduced us to was El Milagro, and they had nine plants. The owner, Manuel Lopez, was very set on using non-GMO corn as he believed that his son got autism from all the trait changes in corn. We did get him started on a high protein white corn that had numerous benefits that were later to be classified as one of the best corns used.

The business involves a lot of hand labor when it comes to doing nursery work or line increases or where we do isolated crossing blocks creating new hybrids. In the fall, there is a lot of hand harvesting. Following harvesting, the corn is dried at a low temperature in drying rooms inside the warehouse.

The corn is dried to 12% moisture and then the nursery material will be hand shelled. During the summer we do hire a lot of part time help to do the hand pollinations in the nursery. Typically, we do set up a field day for a fall demonstration of all the new potential corn hybrids for companies to evaluate.

| Randy and Jo | Darold, Marcia, Jo, Randy | Field Day |

| Doc at the North Farm | Plat Planter with Randy and Braydi |

One of the companies that we did a lot of business with initially was with Tech de AG Mexico. They were a division of Buttonwillow Warehouse Company from Buttonwillow, CA. Their manager was Manuel Sanchez who I have worked with for over 20 years. In many cases, he would bring several customers from Mexico to see the companies' operation and new corn products. In addition, Manuel would bring his ag engineer, Genaro to evaluate the new products. At our annual field day event in the fall, Manuel and Genaro were big contributors to preparing the food with a little authentic Mexican input. It was very good.

Tech Ag de Mexico   Genaro

A large portion of their business was the tortilla industry, so we did concentrate on developing products for that industry. As I had mentioned earlier, Lynn Clarkson had got us started on generating new products for the tortilla industry. It so happens we had developed a high protein white corn hybrid that we decided to have Dr. David Jackson test at the University of Nebraska. He had previously done a 5-year study for the government of Mexico to determine what it would take to produce good tortillas under good economic times and under tough economic times. The nice part of his lab was that the tortillas were the same size as produced in a commercial plant. I informed him that he needed to expand his parameters with this corn as it has 25% more protein than normal corn. He did a great job with the study and the results indicated that we could cook at a lower temperature for 40% less time, and we could reduce the steep time from 14.5 hours to 6.4 hours. Basically, we could double the production of tortillas in a commercial plant.

Dr. David Jackson and William Olson
Food Processing Center
University of Nebraska - Lincoln

Tortillas
Food Processing Center
Univ. of NE - Lincoln

Increased Efficiency in Tortilla Production with High Protein White Corn

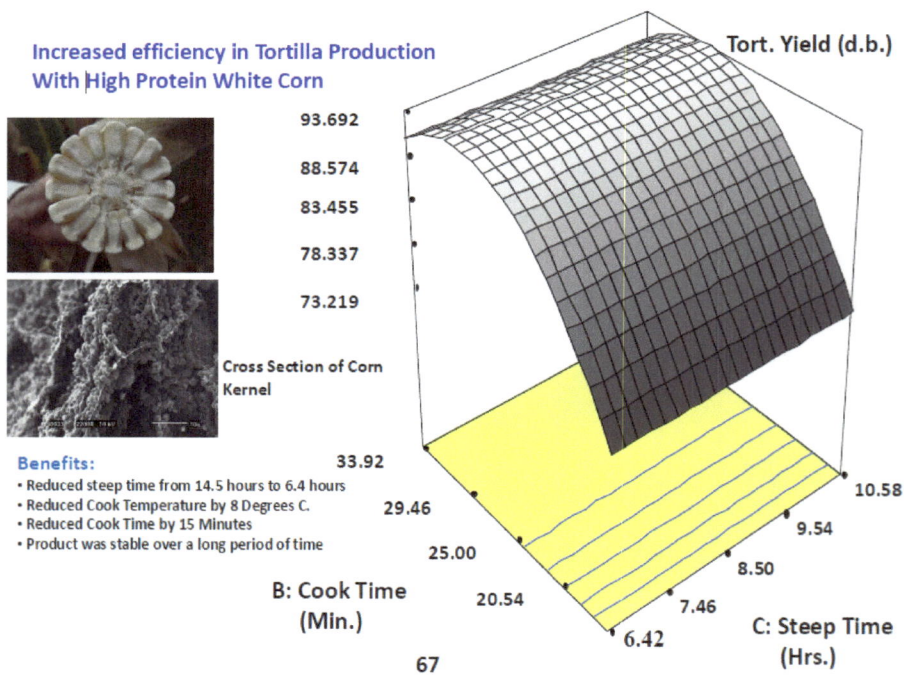

Increased efficiency in Tortilla Production With High Protein White Corn

Tort. Yield (d.b.)

93.692
88.574
83.455
78.337
73.219

Cross Section of Corn Kernel

Benefits:
- Reduced steep time from 14.5 hours to 6.4 hours
- Reduced Cook Temperature by 8 Degrees C.
- Reduced Cook Time by 15 Minutes
- Product was stable over a long period of time

33.92
29.46
25.00
20.54
67

B: Cook Time (Min.)

10.58
9.54
8.50
7.46
6.42

C: Steep Time (Hrs.)

During this same time, we had developed another high protein white hybrid that we had Penford in Cedar Rapids, Iowa test. Penford is a wet mill plant that separates the protein from the starch in corn grain. The starch is used for the paper industry and the food industry. Our purpose was to have them extract the protein so we could use it to replace fish meal in a trout feeding study. The extraction process went very well as they ended up with 2.8 pounds of protein verses their normal 2.2 pounds. We did take the protein to Dr. Ron Hardy at the fish experiment station at Hagerman, Idaho. Dr. Hardy is one of the leading investigators for fish feeding. He did a replicated study on rainbow trout for 12 weeks. The results were very good. The protein had high digestibility (96+%), the filets were whiter, and there was more phosphorus attached to the muscle of the fish. In addition, by using the corn protein, there was 50% less phosphorus used in the diet. All this means is that there is significantly less phosphorus going into the environment and in this case, it would be the Snake River. The fish meal is made from a variety of fish including white fish, anchovies, herring, menhaden, and fileting waste, cannery waste, and other processing waste. Consequently, my using protein from non-GMO white corn, you not only have better quality fish but you lower the level of toxins as the fish meal is a source of contaminates from the ocean. This is a major break through in making healthier food. Currently, all the commercial wet mills are running at full capacity and do not want to take the time to run the new material through their plant. I predict that in the very near future there will be much more attention towards this project.

Trout Filet Testing Results

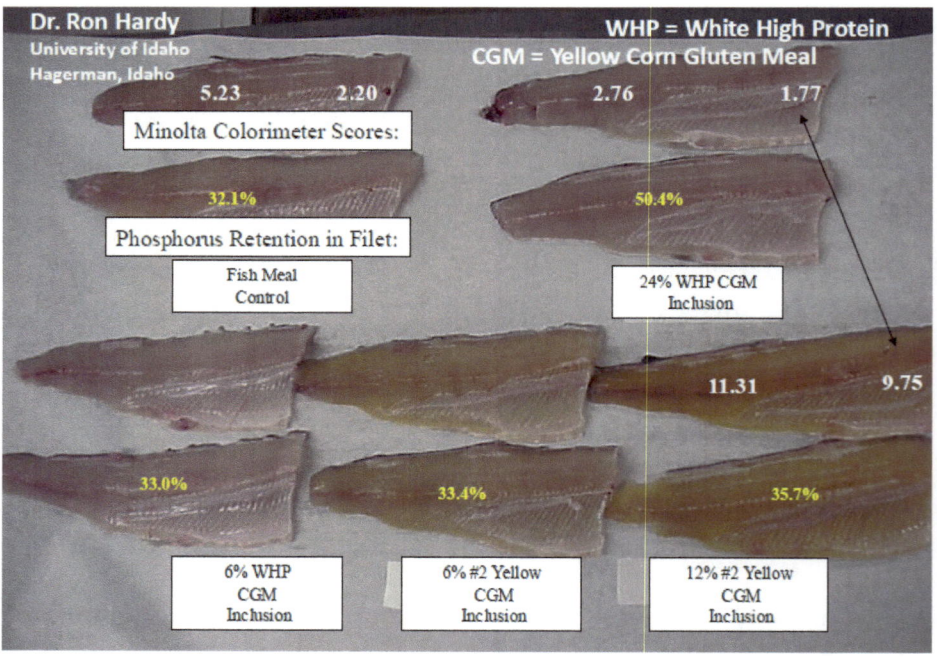

Advantages of Feeding White Corn Protein

1. **Increased Whiteness**

2. **Increased P attached to muscle**

3. **Reduced P to the environment**

4. **Reduced contamination by replacing fish meal**

In addition to the fish and tortilla study, we also conducted a swine study with Land O Lakes as they were part owners of the company, and they had a swine nutrition department that was interested in running a test with the high protein white corn. The trial was conducted on 960 head of hogs with 480 utilizing commercial yellow corn and the other 480 utilizing the high protein white corn. The results indicated that the use of a high protein white corn lowered the feed costs and improved the overall carcass value. It made the fat whiter which was a real plus as Land O Lakes sells a lot of pork to Japan and they prefer the dark colored meat with a bright white fat. Our next step was developing a white corn hybrid that not only had high protein but also had a high oil content. In a feed study with 45 head of hogs being fed this corn verses 45 being fed commercial yellow corn, it was determined that we significantly lowered the back fat and the belly fat. The pictures below tell the story of success better than anything.

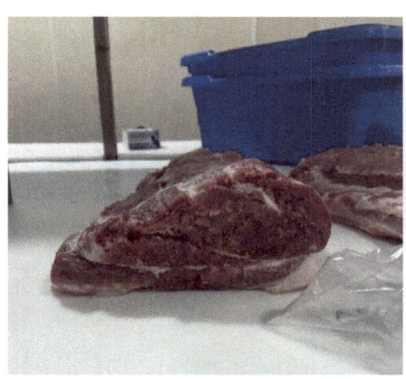

High Protein White Corn

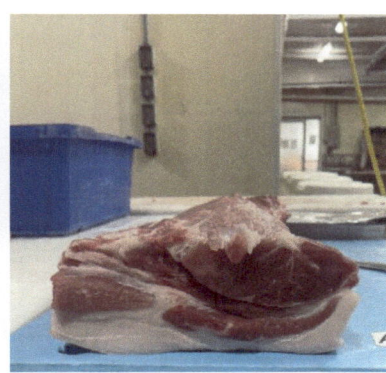

Commercial Corn

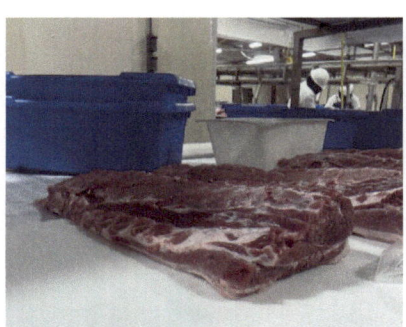

High Protein White Corn

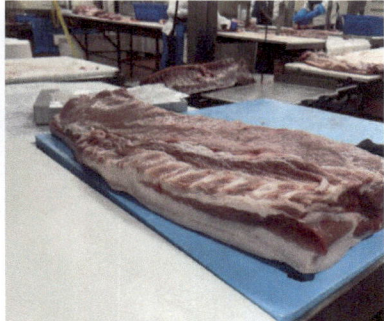

Commercial Corn

A third area of development was with B-H Genetics from Ganado, Texas. The president, Bart Hajovsky, was very aggressive and he had a great plant breeder, Quinton Raab, along with a top-notch agronomist, Travis Janik, to help him with his program. They typically, would do several replicated yield trials in TX, KS, and NE. This really helped us in evaluation of all the new material. Testing is one of the most expensive parts of developing new material.

Basak   Vicki   Ilker

After working with Manuel, Bart, and Lynn for a couple of years, our business got involved with several other entities. We were introduced to Lomo from the ZAAD Company in the Netherlands. They owned a company in South Africa called K2, and a company in Turkey called May Seed. They all had breeders working on corn and were interested in working together. We originally met two of their breeders at the ASTA

Basak   Vicki   Ross

Meeting in Chicago, and from that time on we have exchanged inbred corn lines and made new hybrid combining their material with ours. We also agreed to test the resulting hybrids in the USA and Turkey. So far, the results have been very positive.

The interactions we had with all these contacts have generated some unique opportunities for us in marketing corn genetics and both white and yellow corn hybrids. The company has now reached that stage of development where there have been several proof of concepts completed demonstrating the value of the new products that have been developed. We have been the first company to extract protein from white corn and successfully feed trout and salmon. We have also been the first to create a white corn hybrid with a high protein and high oil combination that has excellent potential for feeding swine and for the extraction of oil for aviation fuel. In addition, we also demonstrated the efficiency of our material in the manufacturing of tortillas. Overall, I could not be more satisfied as to how much we have accomplished with this business.

SUMMARY

I am quite fortunate in that I have had the opportunity to meet many fascinating people from around the world and observe many events during the past eighty plus years. There have been many valuable lessons during that time and hopefully, some of the experiences presented in this book will serve as an incentive for someone to accomplish a goal that may not seem possible at the time. After being paralyzed by polio, I never thought I would be able to travel the country on a motorcycle, or go bowling, snowmobiling in the mountains, or many other things. For this book, I have covered such a long period of time that I have not done justice to all the friends and all the positive interactions I had with them. I would also have to say that meeting so many different people has been not only fun but a valuable learning experience. I would have to think that if people in general, had the positive attitude of trying to work with other nationalities of people, the world would be better off.

I know most will not be interested in all the research items presented in this book, but what we were able to accomplish through the years has been a first in many cases and we would be considered as a non-entity in the minds of all the major seed companies. I am excited to think that my daughter, Vicki, will soon take over the company and take advantage of the opportunities that lie ahead. I cannot overemphasize the importance of maintaining a positive attitude. In 2019, I lost my wife Dorothy to cancer and that was the biggest challenge ever. Fortunately, my daughters, friends and being busy with work helped the situation. I now have a new challenge and that is I have reached the age where I cannot do the things that I would do on a normal basis. I have survived polio, multiple surgeries including a heart valve replacement, fusion of my left ankle, prostate cancer with 42 radiation treatments, high blood pressure, diabetes, two carpel tunnel surgeries, and now an arthritis growth around the spine causing nerve pain in my good leg. As the quest for new and better corn hybrids never ends, I go to work every day.

The value of a good family environment was also one of those factors that one does not realize at the time. It has a strong impact on young people learning how to cope with everyday issues, having someone they can trust and help in making future decisions relating to people, financing, selecting schools or career opportunities.

One of the most important values that I learned from my family was having respect for elders and especially teachers. After meeting with some of the innovative thinkers like my bone doctors, I developed much respect for researchers and older people in general who accomplished so much the years. Today, I work with corn breeders from several countries and they all have something different to contribute to the program. The accumulation of information and the personal interaction is priceless.

The development of a fun hobby is another factor that I not only found useful in handling difficult times, but it was a source of fun and pride in accomplishing something. I think this is one of those hidden factors that also help people deal with retirement. The airplane hobby I had at such an early age has followed me through adulthood. It has made a complete cycle going from model airplanes through today where I am creating corn hybrids with high oil characteristics that will be the source of oil for aviation fuel.

There is also a "Hallmark" like ending to this story. One day I received a letter in the mail from Mary Ann Bartholomew who was living in Oregon and she happened to see my picture on Facebook. Mary Ann was the younger sister of the brothers that I always rode motorcycles with when I was in high school. She is also the granddaughter of James Bartholomew who started the Denison Candy Kitchen in 1913.

At the time of first receiving her letter, she had lost her husband 6 years previously, and Dorothy had been gone 4 years. In both of our previous marriages, we did everything with our spouses. Life then took on a whole different look as it is not fun to go to movies or restaurants by yourself. In my case, my daughter, Vicki, with her six girls and my other two daughters with their family helped a lot. After a lot of letter writing and phone calls, I proposed to her without ever going on a date or taking her out to dinner. For some crazy reason, she accepted my opportunity of a lifetime. She did spend some time in Harlan with the option of not going forward with the wedding if she had second thoughts. She proved to be daring and we proceeded with the wedding. Mary Ann did not want a large wedding, but I had several friends that I wanted to include. We had the wedding at The Harlan Country Club and had my daughter's husband Aaron conduct the ceremony. Mary Ann had Bill Peterson, the son of her previous husband, be her best man. My best man was Randy Gessert who has worked with me for 20 plus years. Two of my granddaughters, Pyper and Sadiee, were also a part of the wedding party. My daughters and their families played a major part in the planning of the whole wedding and the reception that followed.

After almost two years of marriage, I would have to say that we have had a lot of laughs and are enjoying life and each other, taking each day as it comes.

Doc's Daughters

Vicki Mary Ann Doc Jeri Shannon

Key Support Staff

Ross   Randy
Mary Ann   Doc

Mary Ann and Doc

Wedding Party

Bill   Aaron   Randy
Pyper Mary Ann Doc Sadiee

Peterson Family

Jordan Mary Ann Doc   Bill Kim

Appendix A

Herman Strissel	Married	Auguste Wick
(12/6/1849 – 10/22/1890)	↓	(4/20/1857 – 1/19/1920)

Children
- John Ferdinand (6/18/1881)
- William (5/14/1883 – 5/14/1938)
- Herman Carl (4/28/1885 – 11/21/1945)
- Albert (7/3/1886 – 8/16/1962)
- Caroline Marie (11/27/1887 – 2/17/1971)
- Auguste (9/13/1890 – 10/1/1960)

Herman Carl Strissel	Married	Dora Muhl
(4/28/1885 – 11/21/1945)	2/27/1910	(5/8/1877 – 7/3/1942)

Children
- Elsie Strissel (3/2/1911) – 3/19/1911)
- Fritz Herman Strissel (6/22/1917 – 10/14/1993)

Appendix B

Fritz Herman Strissel	Married	Laretta Sophie Marie Arnold
(6/22/1917 – 10/14/1993)	10/12/1939	(7/5/1923 – 4/18/1999)

Children
- Jerry Fred (3/22/1942)
- Judith (twin) (3/22/1942 – 5/18/1942)
- Janet Marie (12/8/1944 – 7/26/1945)
- Daniel Lee (9/20/1947)

Jerry Fred Strissel	Married	Dorothy Jean Lung
(3/22/1942)	7/8/1972	(1/29/1947 – 3/23/2019)

Children
- Shannon Marie (7/4/1974)
- Vicki Lynn (5/14/1976)
- Jeri Renae (7/25/1977)

Jerry Fred Strissel	Married	Mary Ann Bartholomew
(3/22/1942)	5/5/2023	(11/3/1951)